ABDUL AHAD

Want to Be Rich

A Proven System to Earn More, Save Smarter, and Invest Wisely

First edition

This book was professionally typeset on Reedsy.
Find out more at reedsy.com

DEDICATION

To everyone who has ever looked at their bank account with anxiety, wondering if there's a better way to live than paycheck to paycheck.

To the dreamers who refuse to accept that financial stress is just "how life is" and believe they deserve more than constant worry about money.

To the workers who trade their time for money every day while secretly hoping to build something that creates real, lasting wealth.

Contents

Preface

I didn't write this book because I have all the answers or because I've achieved some extraordinary level of wealth that makes me different from you. I wrote this book because I've made every mistake you're probably making right now, felt every anxiety you're feeling about money, and somehow managed to claw my way from financial chaos to financial security through trial, error, and eventually discovering the principles that actually work for building wealth.

Ten years ago, I was drowning in debt with a negative net worth, living paycheck to paycheck despite earning what should have been a comfortable salary, and wondering why I couldn't seem to get ahead no matter how hard I worked. I knew the basics of personal finance; everyone does. Spend less than you earn, invest for the future, avoid unnecessary debt. But knowing what to do and actually doing it are separated by a chasm that swallows most people's financial dreams before they ever get started.

The turning point wasn't discovering some secret strategy that personal finance experts don't want you to know about, because there are no secrets in wealth building. Every strategy in this book has been written about extensively by people smarter and more accomplished than I am. The turning point was realizing that wealth building isn't about having perfect knowledge or ideal circumstances; it's about taking imperfect action consistently over years and decades, making better decisions slightly more often than worse ones, and refusing to give up when progress feels impossibly slow.

I started tracking every expense and finally confronting how much money was disappearing into subscriptions I didn't use, restaurant meals I barely remembered, and purchases that provided no lasting value or happiness. I automated my savings before I had the chance to spend the money, starting with just ten percent of my income when fifty percent felt impossible. I opened my first investment account despite being terrified of making mistakes and losing money in the stock market. I had the uncomfortable conversation with my manager asking for a raise, using a clumsy script I'd practiced a dozen times. I started a side business that earned almost nothing for the first six months before eventually generating meaningful income.

None of these actions felt dramatic or life-changing when I took them. Each one felt small, inadequate, and frankly kind of pointless given how far I needed to go. But small actions compound just like investment returns compound, and a year later I had paid off significant debt, built my first real emergency fund, and started seeing my net worth move in the right direction for the first time in my adult life. Five years later I had eliminated all consumer debt, accumulated six figures in investment accounts, and felt financially secure in ways I literally couldn't imagine when I started. Ten years later I achieved what once seemed impossible: complete financial independence where work became optional rather than necessary for survival.

This transformation didn't happen through brilliance, luck, or extraordinary income. It happened through understanding and implementing the unglamorous basics that this book teaches: earning more through strategic career moves and side income, spending strategically on what matters while ruthlessly cutting waste, investing consistently in low-cost index funds regardless of market conditions, and maintaining discipline through years when progress felt painfully slow. These strategies worked for me despite my mistakes and false starts, and they'll work for you if you actually implement them rather than just reading about them.

The purpose of this book is giving you the complete system I wish I'd had when I started, saving you from the years I wasted on ineffective strategies and the costly mistakes I made through ignorance and poor planning. I've organized everything into a logical progression from mindset through assessment, debt elimination, income maximization, strategic spending, tax optimization, investing, and ultimately creating your personalized wealth plan. Each chapter builds on the previous ones, creating a comprehensive roadmap from wherever you're starting to wherever you want to go financially.

But here's what this book cannot do: it cannot make you wealthy through reading alone, cannot substitute for the uncomfortable actions you'll need to take, and cannot force you to maintain discipline when motivation fades and sacrifices feel burdensome. Those things are on you, and no book can do them for you. What this book can do is remove the excuse of not knowing what to do, provide specific action steps for every phase of wealth building, and offer honest guidance about what actually works versus what sounds good but leads nowhere.

If you're ready to transform your relationship with money, build real wealth over the coming years, and create the financial freedom that changes everything about how you live and work, then turn the page and let's begin. If you're looking for get-rich-quick schemes, secret loopholes, or ways to build wealth without sacrifice and discipline, you should stop reading now and find a different book that will tell you the comfortable lies you want to hear.

The choice is yours. I'm betting you're ready for the truth.

Acknowledgments

This book exists because of countless people who contributed knowledge, support, encouragement, and honest feedback throughout the years it took to write and the decades of experience it draws from.

To my family, who watched me make terrible financial decisions in my twenties, supported me through the difficult years of debt payoff and aggressive saving, never said "I told you so" when my mistakes proved costly, and celebrated every milestone as I built toward financial independence. Your belief in me during the years when I didn't believe in myself made all the difference.

To the mentors and managers throughout my career who taught me about negotiation, career strategy, and the skills that command premium compensation in the marketplace. The raises, promotions, and opportunities you provided or guided me toward created the income that funded everything else in my wealth-building journey. You showed me that my earning potential wasn't fixed and that strategic thinking about career could multiply my income far beyond what annual raises alone would provide.

To the personal finance community, particularly the bloggers, podcasters, and forum participants who openly shared their journeys toward financial independence, making the path visible and achievable rather than mysterious and reserved for others. Mr. Money Mustache, JL Collins, Choose FI, the Bogleheads forum members, and countless others in the FIRE community provided the road map I followed and the inspiration to believe that early financial independence was possible for regular people through disciplined execution of known strategies.

To the early readers who reviewed draft chapters, provided honest feedback about what worked and what needed improvement, challenged my assumptions when I was wrong, and encouraged me to keep writing when the project felt overwhelming. Your input shaped this book in ways large and small, making it clearer, more practical, and more useful than it would have been without your guidance.

To the clients, customers, and employers who paid me over the years, providing the income that I invested to build the wealth I now enjoy. Every dollar I earned from you that I chose to invest rather than spend became part of the compound growth that eventually created financial freedom, and I'm grateful for every opportunity you provided.

To the teachers and authors who wrote the books that taught me about investing, business, negotiation, psychology, and wealth building before I knew enough to even know what questions to ask. Your wisdom compressed into accessible formats allowed me to learn from your decades of experience in days or weeks of reading, accelerating my progress by years or decades compared to learning everything through personal trial and error.

To my accountability partners over the years who checked in on my progress, celebrated wins, commiserated about setbacks, and helped me maintain focus on long-term goals when short-term temptations threatened to derail my plans. Knowing that someone else was watching and that I'd have to report my progress or lack thereof created external motivation that supplemented my internal drive during difficult periods.

To the critics and skeptics who questioned my financial decisions, challenged my strategies, and forced me to think more carefully about what I was doing and why. Your skepticism made me more rigorous in my analysis, more humble about what I didn't know, and more appreciative of the difference between luck and skill in my outcomes.

And finally, to you, the reader, for investing your time and attention in this book and for being willing to consider that your financial future could be different from your financial past. Your decision to read this book and hopefully implement its strategies is the first step toward the financial freedom you deserve, and I'm honored to be part of your journey.

Now let's build some wealth.

Introduction

The Truth About Building Wealth

You've Been Lied to About Money

Everything you've been taught about building wealth is either incomplete, misleading, or designed to benefit someone else at your expense, which is why most people who follow conventional financial wisdom remain stuck in financial mediocrity despite doing what they've been told to do. The lies aren't necessarily malicious, but they're destructive nonetheless, keeping millions of people trapped in cycles of financial stress despite earnest efforts to improve their situations.

You've been told that you need to budget carefully and track every expense, spending hours managing categories and reconciling accounts, when the truth is that most successful wealth builders never budget at all and instead use automation to ensure saving happens first while spending whatever's left guilt-free. You've been told that cutting small expenses like lattes and avocado toast is the path to wealth, when the reality is that your housing, transportation, and food costs matter infinitely more than whether you occasionally splurge on coffee, and optimizing those big three categories creates more wealth in one decision than years of penny-pinching on small pleasures.

You've been told that investing is risky and complicated, requiring expertise to avoid losing everything, when the truth is that simple low-cost index fund investing beats the vast majority of professional money managers and requires no special knowledge beyond the discipline to invest consistently and avoid panic selling during downturns. You've been told that real estate is the only path to real wealth, or conversely that real estate is too risky and stocks are the only way, when the reality is that both can build substantial wealth and the best approach is usually diversifying across multiple asset classes rather than putting everything into one basket.

You've been told that you need to be completely debt-free before investing, paying off every dollar owed before putting a single dollar in the stock market, when the truth is more nuanced: high-interest debt should be eliminated quickly, but low-interest debt like mortgages can often coexist with investing because long-term investment returns typically exceed mortgage interest rates. You've been told that you should max out retirement contributions to get maximum tax benefits, when the reality is that this advice only makes sense after you've eliminated high-interest debt and built adequate emergency funds, because having six figures in a 401k while drowning in credit card debt charging twenty percent interest is financially backward.

You've been told that wealth building is about sacrifice and deprivation, living miserably now so you can enjoy retirement decades from now, when the truth is that strategic spending on what genuinely matters to you while cutting ruthlessly what doesn't creates a life that's satisfying now and building toward freedom later. You've been told that you need significant wealth or income to start investing, waiting until you have thousands or tens of thousands to invest, when the truth is that starting with any amount immediately beats waiting for perfect conditions that never arrive, because time in the market matters far more than timing the market or the size of your initial investment.

These lies and half-truths keep people stuck because they follow advice that sounds reasonable but doesn't actually work for building wealth, spinning their wheels with budgets they can't maintain, saving small amounts while ignoring the big expenses destroying their finances, or avoiding investing entirely because it seems too complicated or risky. Breaking free from these lies requires understanding what actually builds wealth versus what just makes you feel like you're doing something productive.

What This Book Will and Won't Do

This book will provide you with a complete, proven system for building wealth from wherever you're starting, whether that's negative net worth buried in debt or positive net worth ready to optimize and accelerate. It will teach you how to assess your current financial situation honestly without judgment or shame, identify the specific changes that will create the biggest impact on your trajectory, automate systems that make wealth building sustainable rather than dependent on constant willpower, maximize your income through strategic career moves and additional income streams, optimize your spending without miserable deprivation, minimize taxes legally and ethically, invest intelligently in low-cost diversified portfolios, and create your personalized plan with specific targets and timelines.

This book will be honest about the sacrifices, discipline, and time required to build real wealth, acknowledging that the journey takes years or decades of consistent effort rather than weeks or months of intense focus. It will provide specific action steps and frameworks rather than vague motivation or abstract principles, giving you exactly what to do rather than just why you should do something. It will explain the reasoning behind every strategy so you understand not just what to do but why you're doing it, enabling you to adapt approaches to your specific situation rather than blindly following generic advice that might not fit your circumstances.

This book will share my own mistakes and failures alongside successes, showing you the costly errors I made so you can avoid repeating them and the strategies that worked despite my imperfect execution. It will acknowledge the psychological and emotional challenges of wealth building, addressing the fear, anxiety, and discomfort that accompany major financial changes rather than pretending that knowing what to do automatically translates to doing it. It will provide realistic timelines and expectations for different strategies, helping you understand that building one hundred thousand dollars in investments requires different approaches and time frames than building one million dollars.

What this book will not do is promise that you'll be rich quickly, easily, or without significant effort and sacrifice, because those promises are lies that sell books and courses but deliver disappointment and continued financial struggle. It will not provide get-rich-quick schemes, secret loopholes, or strategies that sound too good to be true, because anything that sounds too good to be true in finance is either illegal, extremely risky, or an outright scam. It will not tell you that wealth building is easy or that anyone can do it without effort, because while the strategies are simple, executing them consistently for years requires discipline that many people won't maintain.

This book will not make decisions for you about specific investments, whether to rent or buy in your particular market, or what career moves make sense given your unique skills and situation, because those decisions depend on details about your life that I cannot know from a book. It will not replace professional advice from qualified accountants, financial advisors, or attorneys when your situation requires specialized expertise beyond general wealth-building principles. It will not judge your past financial decisions or current situation, because everyone starts somewhere and what matters is moving forward rather than dwelling on what you should have done differently.

How to Use This Book for Maximum Results

Read this book straight through once to understand the complete wealth-building system and how different components fit together, resisting the temptation to skip ahead to sections that seem most relevant or interesting because each chapter builds on previous ones. Take notes as you read, highlighting strategies that seem most applicable to your situation and marking action items you need to complete. Don't just passively consume the information; actively engage with it by calculating your own numbers, working through the exercises, and answering the questions posed throughout.

After your first complete read-through, return to specific chapters relevant to your current focus area and implement the strategies systematically rather than trying to do everything simultaneously. If you're currently in debt, focus intensively on chapters three and four about debt elimination and income maximization before worrying about optimization strategies in later chapters. If you're debt-free but not investing, focus on chapters ten and eleven about investing basics and portfolio construction. If you're already investing but want to optimize, focus on chapters nine, eleven, and twelve about tax optimization, advanced portfolio strategies, and real estate investing.

Complete the actionable takeaways at the end of each chapter before moving forward, turning knowledge into actual implemented systems and behaviors rather than just theoretical understanding. Set specific deadlines for completing these actions, scheduling time in your calendar to do them rather than hoping you'll get around to them eventually. Share your plans and progress with an accountability partner, whether that's a spouse, friend, or online community member, creating external motivation and support for following through on commitments.

Revisit this book quarterly or annually as your situation evolves, refreshing your understanding of strategies and discovering insights you missed on earlier readings because your context has changed. Use it as a reference when facing specific decisions like whether to buy a house, how to negotiate a raise, or when to transition from employee to entrepreneur, reviewing relevant chapters for guidance rather than making emotional decisions without strategic consideration. Update your personalized wealth plan annually, adjusting targets based on progress and changing circumstances while maintaining focus on long-term financial freedom.

Implement the strategies imperfectly rather than waiting for perfect understanding or ideal circumstances, because wealth built through imperfect action executed immediately far exceeds theoretical wealth from perfect strategies you keep planning but never execute. Start investing with simple index funds even if you don't understand every nuance of asset allocation. Begin tracking expenses with a simple spreadsheet even if you don't have the perfect budgeting app. Ask for a raise using an adequate script even if you haven't perfected your negotiation skills. The learning from doing is far more valuable than additional learning from studying.

Your Invitation to a Wealthy Life

The wealth-building journey you're beginning isn't easy, quick, or guaranteed to succeed, but it's absolutely possible for regular people starting from modest or even negative financial positions to achieve substantial wealth and financial independence through disciplined execution of proven strategies. I know because I did it, starting from negative net worth and crippling debt to achieving financial independence in roughly ten years through the strategies taught in this book. Thousands of others in the financial independence community have done the same, sharing their journeys openly and proving that this path works for people with various incomes, backgrounds, and starting points.

What separates the people who build wealth from the people who remain stuck isn't intelligence, education, or even income level, though higher income certainly helps and accelerates progress. What separates them is the decision to take control of their financial lives rather than passively accepting whatever circumstances provide, the discipline to maintain uncomfortable behaviors for years when progress feels inadequate, and the faith that compound growth will eventually create the freedom they're working toward even when it seems impossibly distant.

You're holding this book because some part of you believes that your financial future can be different from your financial past, that the stress and limitations you've experienced don't have to continue forever, and that financial freedom is possible for you despite wherever you're starting from. That belief is the seed that can grow into actual wealth if you water it with action rather than letting it die through inaction and excuse-making.

The invitation is simple: commit to reading this entire book, implementing the strategies systematically, and maintaining discipline through the difficult years when results feel inadequate compared to effort invested. Commit to progress over perfection, taking imperfect action immediately rather than waiting for ideal circumstances. Commit to the long game, understanding that wealth building is a marathon measured in years and decades rather than a sprint measured in weeks and months.

Your wealthy life is waiting. The only question is whether you'll do what's required to claim it.

Let's begin.

1

The Millionaire Mindset - Rewiring Your Brain for Wealth

Section 1: Your Money Blueprint

Let me ask you something that might make you uncomfortable: What did your parents teach you about money? Think about it for a moment, really think about it, because buried in those memories are the invisible scripts that have been running your financial life on autopilot, perhaps for decades. Maybe you grew up hearing "money doesn't grow on trees" every time you asked for something at the store, or perhaps the phrase "we can't afford that" was the soundtrack of your childhood. These seemingly innocent statements weren't just words; they were programming, deeply embedded code that still influences every financial decision you make today.

The truth is that most of us inherited a money blueprint from our parents, grandparents, and the culture we grew up in, and for the majority of people, that blueprint was designed for survival, not wealth. Our parents taught us what they knew, which was often shaped by their own experiences of scarcity, economic hardship, or simply the middle-class mindset of working hard, saving a little, and hoping it would be enough. This isn't about blaming anyone because our parents did the best they could with the knowledge they had, but it is about recognizing that if you want different results than they got, you need to operate from a different blueprint entirely.

Understanding your current money blueprint requires brutal honesty, the kind that makes you squirm a little in your seat. Take a moment right now and write down every message about money you absorbed growing up, both the spoken and unspoken ones. Did your family stress about bills at the end of every month, creating an association in your mind between money and anxiety? Did you watch your parents argue about finances, unconsciously learning that money causes conflict and pain? Or perhaps you witnessed the opposite, where money was never discussed at all, creating a taboo around the subject that left you feeling ignorant and ashamed about your lack of financial knowledge.

The psychology of poverty versus prosperity isn't about how much money you currently have in your bank account; it's about the operating system running in your mind. Someone with a poverty mindset can win the lottery and be broke again within a few years, which happens to approximately 70% of lottery winners according to various studies. Meanwhile, someone with a prosperity mindset can lose everything and rebuild their wealth from scratch, which is why you see stories of entrepreneurs who went bankrupt multiple times before achieving massive success. The difference isn't luck, intelligence, or even work ethic alone; it's the fundamental beliefs about money, success, and what's possible for someone like them.

Consider the scarcity mindset, which operates from a core belief that there isn't enough to go around, that life is a zero-sum game where someone else's gain must be your loss. This mindset shows up in countless ways throughout your daily life, often so subtle you don't even notice it. You see someone driving a nice car and your first thought is resentment rather than inspiration, assuming they must have gotten lucky, inherited money, or done something dishonest. You hesitate to invest in yourself through education or coaching because you're afraid of losing the money, not considering that the right knowledge could return that investment a hundredfold. You hoard opportunities rather than sharing them, worried that helping someone else succeed might somehow diminish your own chances.

Breaking generational poverty cycles requires more than just earning more money; it demands a complete rewiring of how you think about wealth, success, and your own worthiness to have financial abundance. Many people sabotage their own success because deep down, they don't believe they deserve to be wealthy, or they've internalized the message that rich people are greedy or corrupt. This creates an unconscious conflict where part of you wants financial success while another part actively works against it, ensuring you'll never become the kind of person you've been taught to resent or distrust.

The first step in rewiring your money blueprint is acknowledging that your current financial situation is largely a result of your past programming, not your ultimate potential. You are not your bank account, your credit score, or your current job title. These are simply results, outputs generated by the programming you've been running, and any result can be changed by changing the input. This realization is simultaneously humbling and empowering because it means your past doesn't determine your future, but it also means you must take full responsibility for where you are right now.

Section 2: Beliefs That Build Wealth

Now that we've excavated your old money blueprint, let's talk about installing a new one, the kind that actually creates wealth instead of repelling it. The beliefs you hold about money aren't just abstract philosophical concepts; they're active forces that shape your behavior, your opportunities, and ultimately your results. Every decision you make, from whether to ask for a raise to whether to start that side business, flows directly from these underlying beliefs.

Let's start with perhaps the most destructive belief that keeps millions of people trapped in financial mediocrity: the idea that money is somehow evil, corrupting, or spiritually inferior to being poor. You've probably heard the misquoted saying "money is the root of all evil" countless times, when the actual biblical verse states "the love of money is the root of all evil," which is a completely different message. Money itself is neutral; it's simply a tool, a medium of exchange that amplifies whoever possesses it. If you're a generous person, money makes you more generous because you can help more people. If you're a selfish person, money makes you more selfish because you have more resources to indulge your selfishness. The money isn't the problem; it's the character of the person holding it.

This distinction matters enormously because if you believe money is inherently bad, you will unconsciously avoid accumulating it, sabotaging opportunities for wealth even when they're right in front of you. Your subconscious mind is incredibly powerful and will always move you toward consistency with your deepest beliefs, so if you believe wealthy people are greedy, immoral, or less spiritual than poor people, your mind will ensure you never become one of them. You might start making progress toward financial success only to suddenly make a terrible decision that wipes out your gains, or you might consistently stop yourself just short of the breakthrough that would change everything.

The wealthy mindset understands that money is simply a tool for creating options, security, and impact in the world. With money, you can afford excellent healthcare for your family, education for your children, and the freedom to spend your time on work that matters to you rather than just whatever pays the bills. With money, you can support causes you believe in, help family members in need, and create jobs for others. With money, you can design a life that aligns with your values instead of constantly compromising them for survival. None of this is evil or greedy; it's simply smart and compassionate.

Abundance thinking represents another fundamental shift from the scarcity mindset that keeps most people stuck. Abundance thinking doesn't mean being naive about economic realities or pretending that resources are infinite; it means recognizing that wealth can be created, not just redistributed. When Henry Ford developed the assembly line, he didn't take wealth from someone else; he created it by making automobiles affordable for millions of people who previously couldn't own one. When Steve Jobs created the iPhone, he didn't steal prosperity from others; he generated entirely new wealth by solving problems people didn't even know they had. This is how real wealth is built, through creation and innovation, not through fighting over a fixed pie.

Operating from abundance thinking changes everything about how you approach opportunities and relationships. Instead of seeing other successful people as competition or threats, you see them as proof of what's possible and potential mentors or collaborators. Instead of hoarding information or opportunities, you share freely because you know that helping others succeed doesn't diminish your own potential. Instead of being paralyzed by the fear of losing what little you have, you make bold moves toward what you want because you trust in your ability to create value and generate income.

Delayed gratification mastery might be the single most important skill for wealth building, separating those who achieve financial freedom from those who remain trapped in the cycle of living paycheck to paycheck. The famous Stanford marshmallow experiment demonstrated this principle brilliantly: children who could resist eating one marshmallow in order to receive two marshmallows later showed better life outcomes decades down the road, including higher SAT scores, better health, and greater financial success. The ability to sacrifice immediate pleasure for future gain is essentially the entire game of wealth building distilled into one skill.

Think about every financial decision through this lens of delayed gratification, and you'll immediately see why some people build wealth while others don't. Buying an expensive new car provides immediate pleasure and status, but it destroys wealth through depreciation, high insurance costs, and opportunity cost of what that money could have earned if invested. Investing in index funds provides no immediate gratification whatsoever; in fact, it requires sacrificing money you could spend on fun things right now, but it builds enormous wealth over time through compound growth. Eating out frequently gives you immediate enjoyment and convenience, but cooking at home and investing the difference creates financial margin that compounds into serious money over years.

The challenge with delayed gratification isn't intellectual; everyone understands that saving and investing is smart while overspending is foolish. The challenge is emotional and neurological, as our brains are wired to prioritize immediate rewards over distant ones, a survival mechanism that served our ancestors well when tomorrow wasn't guaranteed but works against us in modern financial life. Training yourself to delay gratification is like building a muscle; it starts difficult and uncomfortable but becomes easier and more automatic with practice. Each time you choose the future benefit over the immediate pleasure, you strengthen that neural pathway and make the next decision slightly easier.

The compound effect extends far beyond money into every area of life, representing one of the most powerful forces in the universe and your greatest ally in building wealth. Compound interest is often called the eighth wonder of the world, and for good reason: it turns small, consistent actions into enormous results given enough time. A twenty-five-year-old who invests just three hundred dollars per month at an average return of ten percent will have over one million dollars by age sixty-five, while someone who waits until thirty-five to start investing that same amount will have less than half that despite only starting ten years later. Those ten years represent hundreds of thousands of dollars in difference, not because of the contributions themselves but because of the compounding growth on those contributions.

Understanding compound growth requires patience and long-term thinking, qualities that are increasingly rare in our instant-gratification culture. We want results now, not in thirty years, which is why get-rich-quick schemes remain eternally popular despite their terrible track record. But the truth is that real wealth is almost always built slowly and steadily through consistent actions compounded over time, not through lottery tickets, day trading, or the next hot cryptocurrency. The people who understand and embrace this truth become wealthy, while those who keep chasing shortcuts remain broke despite occasionally having money pass through their hands.

Section 3: Setting Powerful Financial Goals

Having the right mindset means nothing without direction, without specific targets that transform abstract desires into concrete action plans. Most people have vague wishes about money rather than real goals, hoping they'll somehow "be rich" someday without defining what that actually means or creating a roadmap to get there. This is like deciding you want to take a trip without choosing a destination or planning a route; you'll expend a lot of energy going in circles without making real progress toward anywhere meaningful.

Defining your version of "rich" represents the crucial first step that most people skip entirely, assuming that more is always better without considering what they actually want money to do for them. For some people, rich means never worrying about bills and having the freedom to quit a soul-crushing job. For others, it means traveling the world six months a year or retiring early to spend time with family. For still others, it means building generational wealth that secures their children's and grandchildren's futures or creating a foundation that changes thousands of lives. None of these definitions is more valid than the others, but they require dramatically different amounts of money and completely different strategies to achieve.

Take time right now to envision your ideal wealthy life in vivid detail, not in terms of dollar amounts but in terms of actual daily experience. What time do you wake up, and what do you do with your day? Where do you live, and who do you spend time with? What kind of work do you do, if any, and how much of your time is truly yours to spend as you wish? What experiences do you have regularly, and what do you never have to worry about anymore? This visualization exercise isn't just feel-good fluff; it's strategic planning because you can't hit a target you haven't identified, and you certainly can't create a plan to reach a destination you haven't defined.

SMART goals transform vague wishes into actionable plans by making them Specific, Measurable, Achievable, Relevant, and Time-bound. Instead of saying "I want to be rich," a SMART goal says "I will increase my net worth from negative ten thousand dollars to positive one hundred thousand dollars within five years by earning an additional twenty thousand dollars annually through a side business and investing thirty percent of all income." Notice how this goal tells you exactly what success looks like, gives you a clear time frame, and implies specific actions you'll need to take to achieve it.

Creating your one-year, five-year, and ten-year vision provides both short-term motivation and long-term direction, preventing you from getting lost in daily tactics while losing sight of the ultimate destination. Your one-year goals should focus on foundation building: eliminating high-interest debt, building an emergency fund, increasing income through raises or side hustles, and beginning to invest consistently. These goals should feel challenging but definitely achievable, building momentum and confidence that carries you forward.

Your five-year goals should represent significant progress toward financial independence: a substantial net worth increase, perhaps two hundred thousand to five hundred thousand dollars depending on your starting point; multiple income streams beyond your primary job; a growing investment portfolio that's starting to generate meaningful returns; and dramatically reduced financial stress in your daily life. At this point, you should feel like a completely different person financially than you were five years earlier, operating from security rather than scarcity.

Your ten-year goals should be genuinely life-changing: either complete financial independence where you could stop working if you chose to, or at minimum, enough wealth that money is no longer a primary factor in major life decisions. This might mean a net worth of one to three million dollars, passive income streams that cover your basic living expenses, paid-off mortgage, and the freedom to pursue work you find meaningful rather than just lucrative. This is where the delayed gratification and compound growth of the previous decade pays off in dramatic fashion.

Writing your financial mission statement gives you a North Star to guide decisions when emotions run high and distractions tempt you off course. This mission statement should capture not just what you want to achieve financially but why it matters to you on a deep level. Perhaps your mission is "to build generational wealth so my children never experience the financial stress I grew up with" or "to achieve financial independence by age fifty so I can spend my best years traveling and volunteering rather than sitting in meetings." This mission becomes your anchor when you're tempted to make short-term decisions that conflict with long-term goals.

Your mission statement should be personal enough to genuinely motivate you, specific enough to guide decisions, and meaningful enough to sustain you through inevitable setbacks and challenges. Generic missions like "make a lot of money" won't cut it because they provide no real motivation when things get difficult. But a mission tied to your deepest values, your family's future, your desire for freedom, or your vision for making an impact in the world will pull you forward even when the path gets steep.

Section 4: The Wealthy Person's Daily Habits

Mindset and goals mean nothing without daily actions that reinforce them, turning abstract beliefs into concrete results through consistent habits compounded over time. The difference between wealthy people and broke people isn't usually one big decision; it's thousands of small daily choices that either move them toward financial freedom or keep them trapped in the paycheck-to-paycheck cycle. Understanding this principle is liberating because it means you don't need to make some massive change overnight; you simply need to adjust your daily habits and let compound growth do its magic.

Morning routines of millionaires have been studied extensively, and while the specific activities vary by person, certain patterns emerge consistently across successful people. Most wealthy individuals wake up early, not because they're morning people necessarily but because they understand that controlling the first hour of their day sets the tone for everything that follows. When you wake up with barely enough time to shower and rush to work, you start the day reactive and stressed, letting external demands dictate your focus and energy. When you wake up with margin for intentional morning practices, you start the day proactive and centered, operating from your priorities rather than everyone else's.

A wealth-building morning routine might include thirty minutes of reading or listening to educational content about business, investing, or personal development, which amounts to over one hundred eighty hours per year of learning. It might include exercise that energizes your body and clears your mind for better decision-making throughout the day. It might include meditation or journaling that helps you process emotions and maintain perspective during challenging times. It might include reviewing your goals and visualizing success, programming your reticular activating system to notice opportunities aligned with what you're trying to achieve.

The specific activities matter less than the principle of starting each day by investing in yourself before giving your time and energy to others. This represents the pay-yourself-first principle applied to time rather than money, and it's equally powerful. When you consistently invest in your own growth, knowledge, and well-being first thing each morning, you're essentially depositing into an account that pays compound returns in the form of better decisions, increased opportunities, and enhanced capabilities.

Continuous learning and self-education separate the wealthy from the middle class perhaps more than any other factor because in our rapidly changing economy, your knowledge and skills are your most valuable assets. The wealthiest people in the world are relentless learners, reading an average of fifty books per year compared to just a few for the average person. Bill Gates reads about fifty books per year and credits much of his success to his voracious reading habit. Warren Buffet spends approximately eighty percent of his day reading and thinking, a schedule that seems impossibly leisurely until you realize those habits have made him one of the richest people in history.

You don't need to match this extreme level of reading to benefit from continuous learning; even reading just twenty pages per day amounts to roughly thirty books per year, placing you far ahead of ninety-five percent of the population. The key is consistency rather than intensity, making learning a non-negotiable daily habit rather than something you do occasionally when motivated. This might mean reading during your commute, listening to audio books or podcasts while exercising or doing household chores, or watching educational content instead of mindless entertainment in the evenings.

The subjects you study should focus primarily on skills that increase your earning power and financial intelligence: sales and marketing, business development, investing strategies, real estate, negotiation, leadership, and productivity systems. While reading fiction or philosophy has value, when you're in wealth-building mode, your educational time should be strategically focused on knowledge that directly improves your financial results. You can expand into broader interests once you've achieved financial security, but during the building phase, every hour counts.

Surrounding yourself with success represents another critical habit that shapes your financial future more powerfully than most people realize. Jim Rohn famously said you're the average of the five people you spend the most time with, and research consistently supports this claim. If your closest friends are broke, complain about money constantly, and make poor financial decisions, you'll likely remain stuck in similar patterns regardless of your intentions. If your closest friends are building businesses, investing consistently, and discussing opportunities rather than obstacles, their habits and mindset will naturally influence yours in positive directions.

This doesn't mean you should coldly abandon friends who aren't wealthy, but it does mean you should intentionally cultivate relationships with people who are where you want to be financially or at least heading in that direction. Join local real estate investment groups, attend entrepreneurship meetups, participate in online communities focused on financial independence, or find mentors who've achieved what you're working toward. These relationships provide not just motivation and accountability but also practical knowledge, opportunities, and introductions that can accelerate your progress dramatically.

Accountability systems that work provide the external structure and pressure that complements internal motivation, ensuring you follow through on commitments even when enthusiasm wanes or obstacles arise. Human beings are social creatures who care deeply about reputation and consistency, which makes public commitments and accountability partnerships surprisingly effective at changing behavior. Telling trusted friends or family about your financial goals and regularly updating them on progress creates healthy pressure to follow through, while keeping goals private allows you to quietly give up when things get difficult.

Finding an accountability partner who's also working toward financial goals creates a mutually beneficial relationship where you both benefit from regular check-ins, honest feedback, and shared problem-solving. Schedule weekly or biweekly calls where you report on progress, discuss challenges, and commit to specific actions before the next call. This simple practice transforms abstract goals into concrete commitments and provides immediate consequences for inaction, dramatically increasing your likelihood of following through.

Tracking your progress obsessively might sound tedious, but it's absolutely essential for maintaining momentum and course-correcting before small problems become large ones. What gets measured gets managed, and financial goals are no exception to this principle. Set up a simple system for tracking key metrics weekly or monthly: net worth, monthly income from all sources, monthly expenses by category, savings rate percentage, and investment portfolio value. Watching these numbers improve month after month provides tremendous motivation, while catching problems early prevents minor setbacks from derailing your entire plan.

Creating visual representations of your progress, whether through charts, graphs, or thermometer-style goal trackers, taps into the psychological power of visual feedback and makes abstract numbers feel real and exciting. When you can literally see the line on your net worth graph trending upward month after month, or watch the bar representing your emergency fund grow closer to your goal, the abstract concept of wealth building becomes concrete and tangible. This visualization reinforces positive behaviors and creates emotional investment in continuing the practices that generate results.

Actionable Takeaways

Everything you've read in this chapter means nothing without action, without taking what you've learned and immediately applying it to your specific situation. Knowledge without implementation is just entertainment, so let's translate these concepts into concrete steps you can take today, right now, to begin rewiring your money blueprint and establishing the habits that build wealth.

Money Mindset Assessment Worksheet:
Take thirty minutes today to complete this deep self-reflection exercise that will reveal the invisible beliefs controlling your financial life. Write out honest answers to these questions without censoring or judging yourself:

What did your parents teach you about money, both explicitly and through their actions? List at least ten specific messages or memories. What emotions do you associate with money: excitement, anxiety, guilt, hope, fear, shame, power? What would having more money mean about you as a person, and what negative associations might be blocking your success? If you achieved your financial goals, what would you have to give up or what would change about your identity? What permission do you need to give yourself to become wealthy, and what old beliefs need to die?

Goal-Setting Template:
Use this framework to transform vague desires into specific, actionable plans that actually create results:

My one-year financial goals are (be specific with numbers and deadlines): increase net worth to *X*, earn additional *Y* from side income, reduce monthly expenses by *Z*, begin investing $W monthly. My five-year financial vision is (describe in detail what your financial life looks like): I have *X* in net worth, earn *Y* annually from *Z* income streams, live in a home worth *W* with *V* remaining on the mortgage. My ten-year financial mission is (describe your ultimate financial freedom): I have achieved complete financial independence with *X* in net worth generating *Y* in passive income, allowing me to *Z* with my time.

Thirty-Day Habit Tracker:

Create a simple tracking system for the habits you've committed to building, checking off each day you complete them. Print or create a chart with these habits listed and boxes for each day: wake up by 6:00 AM, complete morning routine including twenty minutes of financial education, track all expenses, review financial goals, avoid impulse purchases over fifty dollars, invest time in side income project, review progress and plan tomorrow.

At the end of thirty days, you'll have clear data on which habits you're successfully implementing and which ones need more attention or different approaches. This tracking alone will significantly increase your consistency because humans naturally want to maintain streaks and avoid breaking patterns once established.

The millionaire mindset isn't something you're born with; it's something you deliberately construct through daily choices, consistent habits, and unwavering commitment to growth. Every wealthy person you admire started exactly where you are now, with dreams bigger than their current reality and nothing but determination to close that gap. The difference between them and the millions who stay broke forever is simply that they committed to the daily practices that build wealth and refused to quit when progress felt slow or obstacles seemed insurmountable.

Your financial transformation begins today, right now, with the decision to stop being a passive victim of your old money blueprint and become the active architect of your financial future. The question isn't whether you can become wealthy; the question is whether you're willing to do the mental work, build the right habits, and maintain consistency long enough for compound growth to work its magic. Everything you need is already within you; now it's time to prove it through action.

2

Financial X-Ray - Know Exactly Where You Stand

Section 1: Your Complete Financial Audit

The moment of truth has arrived, and I won't sugarcoat it: this chapter will be uncomfortable for most people. Looking at your complete financial picture with brutal honesty is like stepping on a scale after months of avoiding it, or checking your credit card statement after a spending spree you knew was out of control. The discomfort you're feeling right now, the urge to skip this chapter and jump ahead to the "exciting" parts about making more money, is exactly why most people never build wealth. They spend their entire lives avoiding the financial reality they've created, hoping it will somehow magically improve without them ever having to confront it directly.

But here's the liberating truth that makes this exercise worthwhile: you cannot fix what you refuse to acknowledge, and you cannot reach a destination if you don't know your starting point. Imagine trying to navigate to a new city without knowing where you currently are; you might drive in circles for years, expending enormous effort while making zero actual progress.

Your financial life works exactly the same way, which is why the wealthy obsessively track their numbers while the broke avoid looking at theirs. This isn't coincidence; it's cause and effect.

Calculating your true net worth represents the single most important number in your financial life, yet most people have no idea what theirs is within even fifty thousand dollars. Your net worth is simply everything you own (assets) minus everything you owe (liabilities), giving you a snapshot of your actual financial position regardless of how much money flows through your accounts. Someone earning two hundred thousand dollars per year but spending two hundred ten thousand has a decreasing net worth and is effectively getting poorer despite their impressive income. Meanwhile, someone earning fifty thousand but spending only thirty-five thousand and investing the difference has an increasing net worth and is genuinely building wealth.

Start by listing every asset you own with its current market value, not what you paid for it or what you wish it was worth. Your primary residence is worth whatever someone would actually pay for it today, which you can estimate using Zillow or recent comparable sales in your neighborhood. Your car is worth its current Kelly Blue Book value, not what you paid or what you still owe on it. Your retirement accounts, investment accounts, and savings accounts are worth whatever the current balance shows. Your personal possessions like furniture, electronics, and clothing are typically worth far less than you imagine, perhaps twenty to thirty percent of what you paid, so don't inflate these numbers with sentimental value.

Now comes the painful part: listing every liability with exact amounts owed regardless of how depressing the totals become. Write down every credit card balance, student loan, car loan, personal loan, medical debt, and mortgage balance with current payoff amounts, not minimum payments or monthly installments. These liabilities represent negative net worth, actual claims against your financial future that are actively preventing you from building wealth. Looking at these numbers probably makes you feel sick, anxious, or ashamed, but remember: awareness is the first step toward change, and you're doing something most people never find the courage to do.

Subtract your total liabilities from your total assets, and there it is: your net worth, the number that reveals your true financial position stripped of all the comforting lies we tell ourselves. If this number is negative, meaning you owe more than you own, you're not alone; millions of Americans are in the exact same position, trapped by student loans, credit cards, and car payments that promised freedom but delivered bondage. If this number is positive but disappointingly small for your age and income, that's actually good news because it means you have income but haven't been deploying it strategically, which is a much easier problem to solve than having no income at all.

Listing every income source forces you to see exactly where money enters your life and identify opportunities to increase that flow. Start with your primary employment income, calculating your actual take-home pay after taxes, insurance, and retirement contributions. Then list every other source of money that hits your accounts: side hustle income, freelance work, investment dividends, rental income, alimony or child support, government benefits, or gifts from family. Most people are shocked to discover they have more income sources than they realized, or conversely, that they're dangerously dependent on a single source that could disappear with one layoff or health crisis.

Calculate your total monthly income from all sources combined, then multiply by twelve to get your annual income. This number represents your current earning power, the raw material you have to work with in building wealth. A higher income certainly makes wealth building easier and faster, but it's not the determining factor in whether you become rich; plenty of high earners stay broke through lifestyle inflation while many moderate earners achieve financial independence through strategic deployment of resources. Your income is simply your starting point, not your destiny.

Tracking every expense for thirty days represents the most revealing financial exercise most people will ever complete, and it's usually disturbing in ways they never anticipated. We all have a mental story about where our money goes, vague notions that rent and groceries consume most of it while everything else is just minor expenses that couldn't possibly add up to much. Then we actually track every dollar for a month and discover that we're spending three hundred dollars monthly on restaurant meals we barely remember, one hundred fifty dollars on subscriptions we rarely use, and two hundred dollars on impulse Amazon purchases that seemed insignificant individually but are devastating collectively.

Use any method that works for you to track expenses: a notebook where you write every purchase, a spreadsheet where you enter transactions daily, or an app like Mint or YNAB that automatically categorizes your spending. The specific tool matters far less than the commitment to capturing every expense without exception, including that two-dollar coffee, that six-dollar lunch upcharge, and that twelve-dollar convenience store stop. These "small" expenses are usually where the most money disappears because we don't think they matter, which is precisely why they matter so much when multiplied by frequency.

At the end of thirty days, categorize your expenses into clear buckets: housing (rent or mortgage, utilities, insurance, maintenance), transportation (car payment, insurance, gas, maintenance, public transit), food (groceries and restaurants separated), insurance (health, life, disability not covered elsewhere), debt payments (minimum payments on all debts), entertainment and recreation, shopping and personal care, subscriptions and memberships, and miscellaneous. Calculate the total for each category and the percentage of your income it represents, creating a clear picture of where your money actually goes versus where you think it goes.

Understanding your financial vital signs means monitoring the key ratios and metrics that reveal your financial health more accurately than any single number. Your savings rate, calculated as the percentage of take-home income you save and invest each month, is perhaps the most important metric for wealth building. If you're saving less than ten percent, you're on the slow track to financial independence that will take forty-plus years. If you're saving twenty percent, you're on the standard track that takes about thirty years. If you're saving fifty percent or more, you're on the fast track that can achieve financial independence in fifteen years or less.

Your debt-to-income ratio, calculated as total monthly debt payments divided by gross monthly income, reveals how much of your earning power is already claimed by past decisions. Lenders typically want this ratio below thirty-six percent, with no more than twenty-eight percent going to housing costs. If your ratio exceeds fifty percent, you're in financial danger territory where one unexpected expense or income disruption could trigger a debt spiral. This ratio helps you understand whether your debt is manageable or crisis-level, and whether you need to focus on debt elimination before other wealth-building activities.

Your emergency fund coverage, measured in months of expenses you could cover with liquid savings, determines your financial resilience and ability to handle life's inevitable surprises without derailing your wealth-building plan. Three months represents the bare minimum for someone with stable employment and good job prospects, six months is better for most people, and twelve months is ideal for entrepreneurs, commission-based earners, or anyone with variable income. Without adequate emergency coverage, every unexpected car repair, medical bill, or home maintenance issue becomes a crisis that forces you into debt, undoing months of progress in a single weekend.

Section 2: The Debt Reality Check

Now that you've faced your complete financial picture, let's talk specifically about debt because it's the single biggest obstacle standing between most people and wealth. Debt is like a heavy anchor attached to your financial boat; you can row as hard as you want toward the island of financial freedom, but as long as that anchor is dragging behind you, your progress will be painfully slow or nonexistent. Understanding debt in all its forms, from the useful to the absolutely devastating, gives you the knowledge to make strategic decisions about which debts to eliminate first and which debts might actually serve your wealth-building goals.

Good debt versus bad debt represents one of the most important distinctions in personal finance, yet most people never learn the difference and treat all debt the same way. Good debt, in theory, is borrowed money that increases your net worth or earning power over time, ideally generating returns that exceed the interest cost of the loan. A mortgage on a primary residence that appreciates in value while you build equity can be good debt, especially at today's historically low interest rates. Student loans for education that significantly increases your earning potential can be good debt, though this is far less true than it was a generation ago. Business loans that allow you to start or expand a profitable business can be excellent debt if managed properly.

Bad debt, conversely, is borrowed money used to purchase depreciating assets or consumable experiences that provide no lasting value or future income. Credit card debt used for restaurant meals, vacations, or shopping sprees is terrible debt, often carrying interest rates of eighteen to twenty-five percent that make it nearly impossible to escape once trapped. Car loans for vehicles worth more than half your annual income are bad debt, especially when you consider that cars lose twenty to thirty percent of their value the moment you drive them off the lot. Payday loans, title loans, and other predatory lending products are catastrophically bad debt with effective interest rates that can exceed three hundred percent annually.

The distinction between good and bad debt isn't always clear-cut in practice because context matters enormously. A mortgage is typically good debt, but not if you bought far more house than you can afford and the payment stress prevents you from investing or building emergency savings. Student loans can be good debt if you finished a degree in a high-paying field, but they're disastrous debt if you dropped out or majored in something with terrible job prospects. A business loan is potentially excellent debt if your business is genuinely profitable, but it's devastating debt if your business fails and you're left with obligations you can't pay.

Listing all debts with complete transparency requires facing numbers that might make you feel physically ill, but this discomfort is necessary medicine for your financial healing. Create a comprehensive debt inventory with these details for every obligation: creditor name, original loan amount, current balance owed, minimum monthly payment, interest rate, and payoff date if you continue making only minimum payments. This complete picture shows you exactly what you're dealing with, how much it's actually costing you, and how long you'll remain trapped if you don't make changes.

For most people, seeing all their debts listed together for the first time is shocking in ways they didn't anticipate. That car loan that seemed reasonable as a monthly payment suddenly looks obscene when you see the total balance and realize you'll pay an extra five thousand dollars in interest over the life of the loan. Those credit cards that felt manageable individually become overwhelming when you see them all together totaling thirty thousand dollars at twenty-two percent interest, which would take twenty-three years to pay off with minimum payments while spending over thirty thousand dollars just on interest. This shock is valuable; let it fuel your determination to escape this trap.

Calculating your debt-to-income ratio reveals whether your debt is a manageable inconvenience or a genuine crisis that requires dramatic action. Add up all your monthly debt payments including mortgage or rent, car loans, student loans, credit cards, and personal loans, then divide by your gross monthly income before taxes. If this ratio is below twenty percent, your debt is probably manageable though you should still focus on elimination. Between twenty and thirty-six percent means you're in the danger zone where debt significantly limits your options and financial resilience. Above thirty-six percent means you're in crisis territory where debt elimination must become your primary financial focus, possibly requiring extreme measures.

Interest rate reality represents the hidden cost of debt that most people dramatically underestimate, focusing on monthly payments rather than total cost and opportunity cost. A thirty thousand dollar car loan at six percent interest over five years doesn't cost thirty thousand dollars; it costs thirty-four thousand eight hundred dollars when you include interest, meaning you paid an extra forty-eight hundred dollars just for the privilege of borrowing money. But the real cost is actually much higher when you consider opportunity cost: if you had invested that four hundred eighty dollar monthly payment instead of sending it to the bank, it would have grown to over forty thousand dollars at ten percent annual returns over the same five-year period.

Understanding this opportunity cost transforms how you think about debt because suddenly that car loan didn't just cost you an extra forty-eight hundred dollars in interest; it cost you over forty thousand dollars in wealth you could have built instead. Credit card debt is even more devastating: a ten thousand dollar balance at twenty-two percent interest, paying just minimum payments of three hundred dollars monthly, will take fifty-nine months to pay off and cost an extra seven thousand six hundred dollars in interest. But if you had invested that three hundred dollars monthly instead, it would have grown to over twenty-three thousand dollars in the same period. That credit card debt didn't just cost you seven thousand six hundred dollars; it cost you over thirty thousand dollars in potential wealth.

This is why debt is the enemy of wealth building, not just an inconvenience or a normal part of life like so many people believe. Every dollar you send to service debt is a dollar that can't compound and grow into your financial freedom. Every month you remain in debt is a month your wealth-building timeline extends further into the future. Every year you spend paying off purchases you made in the past is a year you can't spend building the future you want. Debt keeps you trapped in an endless cycle of working to pay for yesterday while your dreams of financial freedom remain perpetually out of reach.

Section 3: Identifying Money Leaks

Your income might be perfectly adequate to build wealth, but if money is leaking out of your financial boat as fast as it's flowing in, you'll never get anywhere regardless of how much you earn. These money leaks are usually invisible to us because they happen gradually through small decisions that seem inconsequential individually but are devastating collectively. Finding and plugging these leaks often frees up hundreds or even thousands of dollars monthly without requiring you to earn more money or make sacrifices that genuinely reduce your quality of life.

Subscription audits reveal one of the most common and insidious money leaks in modern life, where we sign up for services during free trials or because they seem useful at the time, then completely forget about them while they silently drain our accounts month after month. Pull up your bank and credit card statements for the past three months and highlight every recurring charge, then list them all with their monthly costs. You'll probably find gym memberships you haven't used in months, streaming services you rarely watch, app subscriptions you forgot existed, magazine subscriptions that go straight to recycling, and software subscriptions you signed up for once and never used again.

The psychology behind subscription creep is fascinating and deliberately engineered by companies who understand that people will continue paying for things they don't use rather than going through the minor hassle of canceling. A twelve dollar monthly subscription seems trivial, barely worth the five minutes it would take to cancel, so we let it continue indefinitely despite getting zero value from it. But twelve dollars monthly is one hundred forty-four dollars annually, and if you have ten such subscriptions, that's fourteen hundred forty dollars per year disappearing without providing any benefit whatsoever. That same fourteen hundred forty dollars invested annually at ten percent returns becomes over twenty-five thousand dollars in ten years.

Cancel everything you don't actively use at least weekly, and challenge yourself on the subscriptions you claim to use regularly by asking whether you'd resubscribe if you had to sign up again today. That gym membership you're keeping because you plan to start going again next month probably needs to go, replaced by home workouts or outdoor running until you've proven you'll actually use it consistently. Those streaming services you're keeping "just in case" you want to watch something can be canceled and resubscribed when there's actually something you want to watch, saving you eleven months of payments in exchange for thirty seconds of re-entering your credit card information.

Impulse purchase patterns represent another massive money leak that most people drastically underestimate because they think about each purchase individually rather than as a pattern multiplied by frequency. That twenty dollar shirt you grabbed on clearance without needing it seems harmless, but when you make similar impulse purchases three times per week, that's three thousand dollars annually that literally could have made you wealthy instead. The convenience store stops for snacks and drinks, the online browsing that turns into purchasing, the "treating yourself" because you had a hard day, and the "it's only" purchases that don't seem worth worrying about are collectively destroying your financial future.

Track your impulse purchases separately for one month, defining impulse purchases as anything you bought without planning at least twenty-four hours in advance. This means if you went to the store for milk and came home with forty dollars of other items, those other items were impulse purchases. If you were browsing online and saw something you liked and bought it within minutes of discovering it, that was an impulse purchase. If you stopped at a restaurant because it was convenient rather than because you specifically planned to eat there, that was an impulse food purchase. This tracking will probably horrify you, revealing that hundreds of dollars monthly are escaping through impulses that provide minimal lasting value or happiness.

The latte factor, a term popularized by financial author David Bach, describes how small daily expenses compound into shockingly large amounts over time, yet we dismiss them as too insignificant to matter. A five dollar latte every workday seems like a harmless treat, barely worth worrying about compared to big expenses like rent or car payments. But that daily latte is twenty-five dollars weekly, one hundred dollars monthly, and twelve hundred dollars annually. Invested at ten percent annual returns over thirty years instead of consumed, that latte money becomes over two hundred thousand dollars, enough to fund two years of retirement or buy a vacation home with cash.

The concept applies far beyond expensive coffee to any small recurring expense that's become habitual rather than intentional: daily convenience store stops, frequent takeout meals, morning pastries, afternoon snacks, cigarettes or vaping, lottery tickets, or mobile game purchases. None of these individual expenses will bankrupt you, but collectively they represent thousands of dollars annually that could transform your financial future if redirected toward wealth building. The psychological challenge is that cutting one five dollar latte feels meaningless while the two hundred thousand dollars it could become over thirty years feels abstract and distant, which is why most people keep spending while wondering why they never get ahead.

Emotional spending triggers represent the deepest and most difficult money leak to address because they're connected to our psychological needs, past traumas, and unconscious attempts to fill voids that money can't actually fill. Many people spend money when they're stressed, depressed, anxious, bored, lonely, or celebrating, using purchasing as a temporary emotional regulation tool that provides momentary relief but no lasting solution. Understanding your personal emotional spending triggers is crucial for breaking these patterns and redirecting that money toward actual wealth building.

Spend a week noticing what emotions or situations precede your unplanned purchases, writing down what you were feeling and what happened right before each impulse to spend. You might discover that you online shop when you're bored in the evenings, craving stimulation and the excitement of anticipating packages. You might realize you stop for fast food when you're stressed from work, seeking comfort and convenience rather than actual hunger satisfaction. You might notice you make your biggest purchases after social media scrolling, unconsciously trying to keep up with the seemingly perfect lives everyone else projects online. You might find that shopping trips happen after arguments with your partner, using retail therapy to feel better without addressing the underlying relationship issues.

Once you've identified your triggers, you can develop alternative responses that actually address the underlying need without spending money. If you're bored, call a friend, go for a walk, or start a hobby project instead of browsing shopping sites. If you're stressed, try meditation, exercise, or journaling instead of ordering takeout or making impulse purchases. If you're feeling inadequate from social media, limit your usage and remind yourself that everyone curates their online presence to look better than reality. If you're unhappy in your relationship, have an honest conversation or seek counseling instead of temporarily distracting yourself with purchases that solve nothing.

Replacing destructive financial habits with constructive ones is far more effective than simply trying to stop the destructive behavior through willpower alone. When you feel the urge to make an emotional purchase, pause for twenty-four hours and transfer the amount you would have spent into your savings or investment account instead, creating an immediate positive consequence that rewards delayed gratification. This practice transforms emotional spending from a wealth-destroying habit into a wealth-building trigger, literally turning your weakness into your greatest financial strength.

Section 4: Creating Your Baseline

Everything you've discovered through this painful but necessary financial audit creates your baseline, the starting point from which all future progress will be measured and celebrated. This baseline isn't meant to shame you or make you feel bad about past decisions; it's simply data, accurate information about where you stand right now that allows you to create a realistic plan for where you want to go. Without this baseline, you're essentially trying to navigate without a map or compass, hoping you're making progress but never really knowing whether your efforts are working.

Your starting point snapshot should be documented in detail and dated so you can look back at it months and years from now to see how far you've come. Write down your current net worth, even if it's negative. List your total debt with every balance and interest rate. Record your monthly income from all sources. Document your monthly expenses by category with percentages. Note your savings rate and debt-to-income ratio. List all your accounts with current balances. Take screenshots or print statements so you have proof of your starting point that future you can look back on with pride at the progress made.

Creating a monthly cash flow statement transforms your finances from an overwhelming blur into a clear, manageable system you can understand and control. Your cash flow statement shows every dollar that comes in and every dollar that goes out over the course of a month, revealing whether you're operating in surplus (spending less than you earn) or deficit (spending more than you earn, going deeper into debt). This statement becomes your financial dashboard, the tool you use monthly to monitor progress, identify problems early, and make adjustments before small issues become large disasters.

Your cash flow statement starts with all income sources at the top, showing your total monthly income after taxes. Below that, list every category of expenses with actual dollar amounts, not just estimates or guesses. Calculate your total monthly expenses and subtract them from your total monthly income, revealing your monthly surplus or deficit. If this number is positive, congratulations: you're spending less than you earn and have money available for debt payoff, savings, or investing. If this number is negative, you have an emergency that requires immediate action because you're literally getting poorer every month your spending exceeds your income.

Credit score checks and understanding represent another crucial element of your financial baseline because your credit score affects your ability to borrow money affordably when appropriate and can even impact job opportunities, insurance rates, and housing options. Your credit score is a three-digit number between three hundred and eight hundred fifty that summarizes your creditworthiness based on payment history, credit utilization, length of credit history, types of credit, and recent credit inquiries. Scores above seven hundred forty are considered very good, scores above eight hundred are excellent, and scores below six hundred indicate significant credit problems that need addressing.

Check your credit score for free through services like Credit Karma, your credit card issuer's app, or Annual Credit Report.com which provides free annual reports from all three bureaus. Review your credit report for errors, which are surprisingly common and can unfairly damage your score. Look for accounts you don't recognize that might indicate identity theft, incorrect balances or payment histories, and accounts that should have been closed but still show as open. Dispute any errors immediately through the credit bureau's website, as correcting mistakes can sometimes increase your score by dozens of points overnight.

Understanding what drives your credit score helps you make strategic decisions to improve it over time, which saves money through lower interest rates and better financial opportunities. Payment history accounts for thirty-five percent of your score, making on-time payments the single most important factor; even one missed payment can drop your score by one hundred points and remain on your report for seven years. Credit utilization, the percentage of available credit you're using, accounts for thirty percent; keeping this below thirty percent is good, below ten percent is ideal, which is why paying down credit card balances dramatically improves your score.

Creating your financial dashboard gives you a simple, visual way to monitor your progress without getting lost in overwhelming details or spreadsheet complexity. Your dashboard should include the five to eight most important metrics for your current situation, displayed in a way that makes them easy to track and understand at a glance. For most people in wealth-building mode, this means tracking net worth, monthly income, monthly expenses, savings rate percentage, total debt balance, emergency fund balance, and investment account value.

Update your dashboard monthly on the same day each month, perhaps the first of the month or the day after payday, creating a ritual that keeps you connected to your finances and aware of your progress. Watching your net worth increase month after month provides tremendous motivation to continue the behaviors creating that growth. Seeing your debt balance decrease steadily reinforces that your sacrifices are working and freedom is approaching. Observing your investment account grow even when you're not actively adding money demonstrates the power of compound returns and market growth working on your behalf.

The psychological impact of tracking cannot be overstated; what gets measured gets managed, and what gets managed gets improved. By simply paying attention to your financial numbers and monitoring them regularly, you'll naturally make better decisions without requiring superhuman willpower or discipline. When you know you're checking your spending at the end of the month, you'll think twice before making impulse purchases. When you see your savings rate percentage, you'll feel motivated to find ways to increase it. When you watch your net worth grow, you'll feel proud and excited rather than anxious and ashamed about money.

Actionable Takeaways

This chapter has given you a complete framework for understanding your current financial reality, but understanding means nothing without implementation. The difference between people who transform their finances and people who stay stuck forever is simply that the successful ones actually do the work, completing these exercises fully and honestly rather than skipping ahead or doing them halfway. Commit right now to completing every single takeaway this week, and you'll have accomplished more toward financial freedom than most people manage in years.

Net Worth Calculator Spreadsheet:

Create a comprehensive net worth tracking system that you'll update monthly for the rest of your wealth-building journey. Set up a simple spreadsheet with three main sections: Assets, Liabilities, and Net Worth. Under Assets, list every account and possession: checking account, savings account, retirement accounts, investment accounts, home value, car value, and other significant possessions. Under Liabilities, list every debt: mortgage balance, car loans, student loans, credit cards, personal loans, and medical debt. Calculate your net worth by subtracting total liabilities from total assets, and date this entry as your baseline.

Expense Tracking Template:

For the next thirty days minimum, track every single expense without exception using whatever method works best for your habits and preferences. Download an app like Mint or YNAB if you want automation, create a spreadsheet if you prefer manual tracking with more control, or simply use a notebook if you want the lowest-tech solution. The key is capturing every expense, from your mortgage payment to that two-dollar candy bar, because the small recurring expenses you think don't matter are often where the most money disappears.

Debt Inventory Worksheet:

Create a complete debt inventory listing every obligation with full details: creditor name, total balance owed, interest rate, minimum monthly payment, and projected payoff date if you continue making only minimum payments. Calculate your total debt across all obligations and your total monthly debt payments. Determine your debt-to-income ratio by dividing total monthly debt payments by gross monthly income. This worksheet becomes your road map for debt elimination, showing you exactly what you're fighting against and tracking your victories as balances decrease.

Financial Health Scorecard:

Assess your current financial health across multiple dimensions, giving yourself an honest grade in each category: net worth for your age and income (are you where you should be?), debt levels (manageable or crisis?), emergency fund adequacy (months of expenses covered), savings rate (percentage of income saved monthly), credit score (excellent, good, fair, or poor), income diversification (single source or multiple streams), and insurance coverage (adequately protected or vulnerable). This scorecard identifies which areas need immediate attention and which are already strong, allowing you to prioritize your efforts strategically.

The discomfort you felt reading this chapter and completing these exercises is proof that you're doing something most people never find the courage to do: facing your financial reality with complete honesty. This discomfort is temporary, but the clarity and control you've gained through this process will transform your financial life permanently. You now know exactly where you stand, what you're working with, and what needs to change, which means you're no longer stumbling in the dark hoping things will magically improve.

Your financial baseline isn't something to be ashamed of regardless of how dire it might look; it's simply the starting point of your wealth-building journey, and every successful person started from their own version of ground zero. What matters now isn't where you've been or what financial mistakes you've made; what matters is what you do next, armed with complete knowledge of your situation and clear direction forward. The path from here to financial freedom is visible now, and every step you take from this point on moves you measurably closer to the life you want.

3

Debt Freedom - Your First Wealth Milestone

Section 1: The Debt Elimination Strategy

Debt freedom represents the first major milestone on your journey to wealth, the moment when you break free from the chains that have been holding you back and can finally redirect your full financial power toward building instead of paying for the past. For most people reading this book, debt elimination will be the hardest part of their entire wealth-building journey because it requires sustained sacrifice, unwavering discipline, and the emotional fortitude to keep fighting when progress feels painfully slow. But it's also the most trans formative part because the psychological shift that happens when you make that final debt payment and realize you're truly free is worth more than the actual dollars involved.

Understanding why debt elimination must come first, before aggressive investing or building multiple income streams or any other wealth-building strategy, requires recognizing the mathematics of interest rates and opportunity cost. If you're carrying credit card debt at twenty percent interest while trying to invest in the stock market for an average ten percent return, you're literally losing ten percent on every dollar you invest instead of using for debt payoff. This isn't just suboptimal; it's actively destructive, like trying to fill a bathtub while the drain is wide open. You might eventually succeed if you pour enough water, but you'd achieve the result much faster by simply closing the drain first.

The debt avalanche method represents the mathematically optimal approach to debt elimination, focusing your extra payments on the highest interest rate debt first while making minimum payments on everything else. This strategy saves you the most money in interest charges and gets you out of debt fastest according to pure mathematics, which is why financial experts almost universally recommend it. You list all your debts from highest to lowest interest rate, attack the top one with every extra dollar you can find until it's eliminated, then move to the next highest rate while rolling the payment from the eliminated debt into the new target.

Here's how the avalanche method works in practice: imagine you have a credit card with a five thousand dollar balance at twenty-two percent interest, a car loan with fifteen thousand dollars remaining at six percent interest, and a student loan with twenty-five thousand dollars at four percent interest. Your minimum payments are one hundred fifty dollars on the card, three hundred fifty dollars on the car, and two hundred dollars on the student loan, totaling seven hundred dollars monthly. You find an extra three hundred dollars in your budget through side income and expense cutting, giving you one thousand dollars total to throw at debt each month.

Using the avalanche method, you'd put four hundred fifty dollars toward the credit card (minimum plus extra three hundred), three hundred fifty toward the car, and two hundred toward the student loan. Within twelve months, that credit card would be completely gone, saving you years of interest payments. Then you'd roll that four hundred fifty dollar payment into the car loan, now paying eight hundred dollars monthly on it while maintaining the two hundred dollar student loan payment. The car loan would be eliminated in about twenty-one months total from when you started. Finally, you'd roll everything into the student loan, paying one thousand dollars monthly and eliminating it in about twenty-eight months total. Your entire debt would be gone in under two and a half years, and you'd have saved thousands in interest compared to just making minimum payments forever.

The debt snowball method takes a different approach, focusing on psychological wins rather than mathematical optimization by targeting your smallest debt balance first regardless of interest rate. This method, popularized by Dave Ramsey, acknowledges that personal finance is more about behavior and psychology than pure mathematics, and that many people need the motivation of quick wins to maintain momentum through the long slog of debt elimination. You list all debts from smallest to largest balance, attack the smallest one first with all extra money until it's gone, then roll that payment into the next smallest debt, creating a "snowball" effect as your available payment amount grows with each eliminated debt.

Using the same debts from the previous example but with the snowball method, you'd attack them in different order based purely on balance size. If that credit card actually had the smallest balance despite the highest interest rate, you'd still start there, but if your student loan had a small balance of say three thousand dollars while the credit card was larger, you'd start with the student loan first. The psychological power of eliminating an entire debt quickly, even if it's the lowest interest rate, cannot be understated for many people who need those emotional victories to stay motivated over months or years of sacrifice.

Which method is right for you depends entirely on your personality and what will keep you engaged in the debt elimination process long enough to finish. If you're highly analytical and motivated by saving the maximum amount of money, the avalanche method is clearly superior and will get you debt-free faster while spending less on interest. If you're someone who needs frequent wins and positive reinforcement to maintain motivation, the snowball method might actually get you better results despite being less mathematically optimal, because you'll stick with it instead of giving up when progress feels too slow.

The brutal truth that most personal finance gurus won't tell you is that the best debt elimination method is whichever one you'll actually complete, because starting the mathematically optimal approach and quitting after six months leaves you worse off than using the sub optimal approach but fighting through to debt freedom. There's no shame in choosing the snowball method if you know yourself well enough to recognize that you need those quick wins to maintain emotional investment in the process. The only wrong choice is doing nothing or giving up halfway through because progress feels too slow or the sacrifices feel too hard.

Combining elements of both methods creates a hybrid approach that might work even better for your specific situation. Start with the snowball method to get a quick win and build momentum, knocking out your smallest debt within the first few months to prove to yourself that this is actually working. Then switch to the avalanche method for the remaining debts, tackling the highest interest rates first now that you've built confidence and momentum. This hybrid approach gives you the psychological boost of an early victory while still optimizing for minimum interest paid on the larger debts that will take longer to eliminate.

Section 2: Negotiating Your Way to Freedom

Most people don't realize that debt is often negotiable, that you're not necessarily stuck with the interest rates and terms you originally agreed to, and that creditors would often rather accept reduced payments or settlements than risk getting nothing if you default or declare bankruptcy. Understanding negotiation principles and having the courage to actually make those calls can save you thousands of dollars and shave months or even years off your debt elimination timeline. The worst thing a creditor can say is no, leaving you exactly where you started, but they might say yes and transform your financial situation overnight.

Negotiating lower interest rates on credit cards is one of the easiest and most effective negotiations you can have, often requiring nothing more than a simple phone call and fifteen minutes of your time. Credit card companies want to keep you as a customer, especially if you have a history of making payments, and they have significant flexibility to adjust your rate if it means retaining your business. Call your credit card company and simply say you've been offered a lower rate elsewhere and you're considering transferring your balance unless they can match or beat that rate. You don't actually need to have another offer; this is standard negotiating language that customer service representatives hear constantly.

Here's a script you can use almost word-for-word: "Hello, I've been a customer for X years and I've always made my payments on time. I'm currently paying Y percent interest on my balance, and I've received offers for cards with much lower rates around Z percent. I'd prefer to keep my account with you since I've been happy with your service, but I need a lower rate to make that work financially. Can you reduce my interest rate to something more competitive?" This script is polite but firm, expressing loyalty while making clear that you have alternatives and you're willing to leave if they don't accommodate you.

Approximately half of people who call and ask for lower rates receive them, according to various surveys, yet only about twenty percent of cardholders ever bother to ask. This means millions of people are paying thousands of dollars in unnecessary interest simply because they never thought to make a phone call, or they assumed it wouldn't work, or they felt uncomfortable asking. Overcome that discomfort because a fifteen-minute phone call that reduces your rate from twenty-two percent to fifteen percent on a ten thousand dollar balance saves you over five hundred dollars in the first year alone and helps you eliminate the debt months faster.

If your first call doesn't work, don't give up; call back and speak with a different representative who might be more willing or able to help. If you're repeatedly denied, ask to speak with a supervisor or retention specialist, as these individuals often have more authority to make deals. If your card company absolutely refuses to negotiate, follow through on your threat and transfer your balance to a card with a lower rate or a zero percent balance transfer offer, immediately saving hundreds in interest. Just be careful about balance transfer fees, which typically run three to five percent of the transferred amount and can eat into your savings if you're not careful with the math.

Balance transfer strategies can be incredibly powerful for debt elimination when used correctly, moving high-interest debt to zero percent or low-interest promotional offers and using the interest-free period to aggressively pay down principal. Many credit cards offer twelve to twenty-one months of zero percent interest on balance transfers, giving you a window to make serious progress without interest charges adding to your burden. A ten thousand dollar credit card balance at twenty-two percent interest requires a monthly payment of about three hundred thirty dollars just to pay off in three years, with over two thousand five hundred dollars going to interest. Transfer that same balance to a zero percent card and that same three hundred thirty dollar monthly payment eliminates the entire debt in about thirty months with zero dollars wasted on interest.

The catch with balance transfers is that they almost always come with transfer fees of three to five percent of the balance, so transferring ten thousand dollars might cost you three hundred to five hundred dollars upfront. You need to do the math to ensure the transfer fee is less than the interest you'd pay by leaving the balance where it is, which is almost always true if you're transferring from a high-interest card and you have a solid plan to eliminate the debt during the promotional period. The trap that catches many people is transferring the balance and then failing to pay it off before the promotional rate expires, at which point you're hit with a potentially even higher interest rate on the remaining balance plus you've wasted the transfer fee.

Debt consolidation loans represent another option for simplifying multiple debts into one payment with potentially lower overall interest, but they come with significant risks that make them a poor choice for many people. The concept is straightforward: you take out a personal loan at a hopefully lower interest rate than your credit cards and use it to pay off all your existing debts, leaving you with just one monthly payment instead of juggling multiple creditors. When it works, this strategy saves money on interest and simplifies your financial life, making it easier to stay organized and focused on elimination.

The problems with debt consolidation become apparent when you understand how most people actually use these loans compared to how they're supposed to be used. The loan pays off your credit cards, bringing all those balances to zero, which feels like a fresh start and tremendous relief. But then, with all that newly available credit and the psychological sense that the problem is solved, many people start using those cards again, running up new balances on top of the consolidation loan payment. Within a year or two, they have both the consolidation loan payment and new credit card debt, leaving them in worse financial shape than before they consolidated. Studies show that approximately seventy percent of people who consolidate debt end up in more debt within a few years, which is a terrible success rate and should make you very cautious about this approach.

If you're going to consider debt consolidation, you must commit to destroying your credit cards or at least removing them from your wallet and freezing them in a block of ice in your freezer so you can't use them impulsively. The consolidation only works if it's part of a genuine behavior change where you stop using debt entirely, not just a temporary relief that lets you continue destructive financial habits with a cleaner slate. Without that behavior change, consolidation just extends your debt servitude and wastes the money you pay in origination fees and interest on the consolidation loan itself.

Settlement options for overwhelming debt become relevant when your debt load is so crushing that you realistically cannot pay it all back through normal means, typically when you owe more than fifty percent of your annual income in unsecured debt and you're already behind on payments or about to be. Debt settlement involves negotiating with creditors to accept less than the full balance owed, often thirty to fifty percent of the original debt, in exchange for a lump sum payment or structured settlement. This approach severely damages your credit and should be considered only as a last resort before bankruptcy, but it can provide a path forward when you're otherwise completely stuck.

The debt settlement process typically works through a settlement company, though you can attempt to negotiate directly with creditors yourself if you have the emotional fortitude and negotiation skills. You stop making payments to creditors and instead deposit money into a dedicated settlement account monthly, building up funds that will eventually be used to make settlement offers. As accounts go delinquent and charge-off, typically after six months of non-payment, the settlement company negotiates with creditors or collection agencies to accept a fraction of the balance as payment in full. This process is emotionally brutal, destroys your credit, subjects you to constant collection calls, and takes two to four years to complete, but it eliminates debt that would otherwise take decades to pay off through minimum payments.

The costs and risks of debt settlement are substantial and must be fully understood before going down this path. Settlement companies typically charge fees of twenty to twenty-five percent of your enrolled debt, so settling fifty thousand dollars in debt might cost you ten thousand to twelve thousand dollars in fees alone. Your credit score will plummet as accounts go delinquent, making it difficult or impossible to get new credit, rent apartments, or sometimes even get hired for certain jobs that check credit. You may face lawsuits from creditors before settlements are reached, adding legal stress to an already difficult situation. And crucially, forgiven debt is typically considered taxable income by the IRS, so if you settle thirty thousand dollars in debt for ten thousand, you may owe taxes on the twenty thousand dollars of forgiven debt, creating a surprise tax bill when you file your return.

Despite these serious downsides, debt settlement makes sense for people who are truly drowning and have no realistic path to paying off their debt through conventional means. If you're facing bankruptcy anyway, settlement might allow you to avoid that more severe consequence while still getting out from under crushing debt. If your choices are realistically between settlement and never escaping debt for decades while making minimum payments, settlement provides an escape route despite its costs. Just understand that this is major financial surgery with serious side effects, not something to consider lightly or before exhausting all other options.

Section 3: Extreme Debt Payoff Tactics

Normal debt elimination approaches work fine if you have manageable debt levels and reasonable income, but sometimes your situation requires extreme measures that go beyond cutting cable and making coffee at home. When you're tens of thousands in debt and the standard advice feels laughably inadequate, you need to consider strategies that involve significant sacrifice and dramatic lifestyle changes that will be temporary but trans formative. These extreme tactics can shave years off your debt elimination timeline and free you to start building wealth much sooner, but they require a level of commitment and intensity that most people won't sustain.

Selling stuff you don't need is the fastest way to generate immediate cash for debt payoff while simultaneously simplifying your life and breaking emotional attachments to possessions that may be part of your financial problems. Most American households have thousands of dollars worth of unused items sitting in closets, garages, and storage units, things they haven't touched in years but keep "just in case" or because of sentimental value or simple inertia. Walk through your home with ruthless honesty and identify everything you could live without: extra vehicles, recreational equipment you rarely use, electronics gathering dust, furniture in storage, clothing you never wear, tools you don't need, collectibles that aren't bringing you joy, and any other possessions that could be converted to cash and thrown at debt.

The psychology of selling possessions is more complex than it seems because we attach meaning and identity to our stuff beyond its actual utility or value. That motorcycle sitting in your garage represents freedom and adventure even though you've ridden it twice in three years, so selling it feels like giving up on dreams rather than eliminating a depreciating asset that costs you insurance and maintenance. Those golf clubs represent the lifestyle you want to have even though you play once a year, so selling them feels like admitting defeat rather than acknowledging reality. That designer handbag collection represents status and taste even though the bags sit unused while costing you thousands that could eliminate debt, so selling feels like losing part of your identity rather than converting unnecessary luxury to debt freedom.

Breaking through this psychological resistance requires brutal honesty about the difference between the life you're living and the life you tell yourself you're living. You're not a motorcyclist if you ride twice a year; you're someone who owns an expensive motorcycle. You're not a golfer if you play once annually; you're someone with expensive clubs in storage. You're not deriving meaningful value from possessions you don't use; you're just storing them at tremendous opportunity cost while debt keeps you trapped in financial stress. Selling these items won't take away your identity or your dreams; it will fund your freedom so you can eventually afford to pursue those interests for real rather than just own the props that signal them.

Use online marketplaces like Facebook Marketplace, Craigslist, OfferUp, and eBay to sell items quickly, pricing aggressively to move inventory rather than holding out for maximum value. The goal isn't to get the best possible price; the goal is to convert unused possessions to debt payoff funds as quickly as possible. A thousand dollars from selling stuff today is worth more than fifteen hundred dollars from selling the same stuff over six months because that thousand dollars immediately stops accruing interest on your debt. Have a massive garage sale and advertise it widely, pricing everything to sell and accepting reasonable offers because every dollar raised is a dollar closer to freedom.

Side hustle income dedicated entirely to debt payoff represents perhaps the most powerful wealth-building strategy available because it attacks the problem from the income side rather than just cutting expenses, creating extra money that didn't exist before and directing it with laser focus toward debt elimination. Every dollar of side income thrown at debt has triple impact: it reduces your principal balance, stops interest from accruing on that portion of debt, and accelerates your debt freedom date. An extra five hundred dollars monthly in side income dedicated to debt can eliminate twenty thousand dollars of debt years faster than minimum payments alone, transforming a decade of debt servitude into just a few intense years.

The key to sustainable side hustling during debt elimination is choosing work that leverages your existing skills, doesn't require significant upfront investment, and can be done on your own schedule around your primary job and family obligations. Freelancing in your professional skill area is often the most lucrative option: writing, graphic design, web development, consulting, bookkeeping, or any service you already know how to provide professionally. Local service businesses like lawn care, house cleaning, pet sitting, or handyman work can generate solid income with minimal startup costs if you're willing to do physical labor. Gig economy work like Uber, DoorDash, Instacart, or Task Rabbit provides ultimate flexibility though often at lower hourly rates than skilled freelancing.

Calculate your side hustle income on an hourly basis to ensure you're using your time efficiently and not just creating busy work that barely moves the needle on your debt. If you're making twelve dollars per hour after expenses driving for Uber, but you could make fifty dollars per hour freelancing in your professional skill, you're wasting your limited time and energy on the less productive option. There's nothing wrong with gig work if it's genuinely your best option, but most people with professional skills can earn far more by monetizing those skills through freelancing than by doing unskilled gig work.

The critical difference between side hustling to fund lifestyle versus side hustling to eliminate debt is that every penny of debt elimination side income must go directly to debt with zero diversion to spending or consumption. Set up automatic transfers so your side income goes immediately to debt payments rather than mixing with your primary income where it might get spent on regular expenses. Treat side income as if it doesn't exist for anything except debt payoff, maintaining your normal budget from your primary job and using the side income purely as a debt destruction weapon. This psychological separation helps you sustain the intensity because you're not sacrificing your normal lifestyle; you're just working extra to escape debt faster.

The "no spend" challenge represents an extreme but effective tactic where you commit to spending nothing beyond absolute necessities for a defined period, typically thirty to ninety days, redirecting every saved dollar toward debt elimination. During a no spend challenge, you can spend on housing, minimum debt payments, basic groceries, utilities, insurance, and other true necessities, but everything discretionary is completely off limits: no restaurant meals, no entertainment expenses, no shopping for anything except essentials, no convenience purchases, and no "treating yourself" for any reason. This creates forced savings of hundreds or even thousands of dollars that might normally leak away through small discretionary spending.

No spend challenges are mentally difficult but often surprisingly trans formative because they break consumption habits and reveal how much money you've been wasting without realizing it. The first week is hardest as you confront boredom, social pressure, and ingrained spending habits without your usual escape valves of shopping or eating out. The second week gets easier as you develop new routines and find free alternatives to paid entertainment. By week three, you often discover that you don't miss most of the spending you thought was essential, and you might even feel liberated by the simplicity of not making constant purchasing decisions.

Many people who complete a no spend challenge find that their spending remains permanently lower even after the challenge ends because they've broken the autopilot consumption habits that were draining their finances. They realize they don't actually need restaurant meals multiple times per week, that free entertainment options are plentiful if you look for them, and that most impulse purchases were filling emotional needs rather than genuine practical ones. This attitude shift is worth as much as the immediate debt payoff benefit because it changes your relationship with money and consumption long-term.

Lifestyle downgrade strategies involve temporarily accepting a significantly lower standard of living than you can technically afford, redirecting the difference between what you're currently spending and what you could survive on toward aggressive debt elimination. This might mean moving from a nice apartment to a cheaper one or getting roommates to split housing costs, trading your expensive car for a reliable beater that costs a fraction in payments and insurance, cutting your grocery budget to rock-bottom levels through meal planning and bulk buying, eliminating all entertainment subscriptions and memberships, and generally living like a broke college student despite earning a decent income.

The psychological challenge with lifestyle downgrade is that it feels like going backward in life, losing status and comfort you've worked hard to achieve, admitting to yourself and others that you're not as financially successful as you appeared. This is especially hard for people in their thirties and forties who are watching peers buy homes and upgrade their lifestyles while they're moving in the opposite direction. But this temporary sacrifice is the price of past financial mistakes, and the faster you accept that and embrace the downgrade, the faster you get through it and emerge on the other side debt-free and able to build real wealth rather than the fake wealth of borrowed money funding a lifestyle you can't afford.

The math of extreme lifestyle downgrade is undeniable: if you're currently spending three thousand dollars monthly beyond debt payments and you cut that to fifteen hundred through strategic downgrades, you've just found fifteen hundred dollars monthly for debt payoff. That fifteen hundred dollars monthly eliminates fifty thousand dollars in debt in about three years depending on interest rates, turning a fifteen-year debt burden into a three-year intense sprint. Three years of sacrifice to escape fifteen years of debt servitude is an obviously good trade, yet most people won't make it because they prioritize current comfort over future freedom, staying stuck in debt forever rather than accepting temporary discomfort for permanent improvement.

Section 4: Staying Debt-Free Forever

Eliminating debt is only half the battle; staying debt-free forever requires building new habits and systems that prevent you from falling back into the trap that caught you the first time. Most people who successfully eliminate debt eventually slide back into it within a few years because they never addressed the underlying behaviors and situations that created the problem, treating the symptom while ignoring the disease. Understanding how to prevent debt recurrence is just as important as learning how to eliminate existing debt because you don't want to fight this battle twice.

Emergency fund basics represent your first line of defense against falling back into debt because unexpected expenses are inevitable and you need a buffer to handle them without resorting to credit cards. Financial experts debate whether you should build an emergency fund while paying off debt or focus exclusively on debt elimination, and the answer depends on your specific situation and risk tolerance. At minimum, you need a small starter emergency fund of one thousand dollars before beginning aggressive debt payoff, providing basic protection against small emergencies like car repairs or medical copays without derailing your entire plan.

The logic behind the starter emergency fund rather than waiting until debt elimination is complete acknowledges human psychology and the reality that emergencies will happen whether you're ready or not. If you have zero emergency savings and aggressive debt payoff is consuming all your extra income, what happens when your car breaks down or your kid needs an emergency dental procedure? You go right back into credit card debt, undoing months of progress and often giving up on debt elimination entirely out of frustration and despair. That small thousand-dollar buffer prevents this scenario, giving you basic protection while you focus intensity on debt.

Once you're debt-free, building a full emergency fund of three to six months of expenses becomes your top priority before beginning aggressive investing or other wealth-building activities. This substantial cushion protects you against major emergencies like job loss, serious medical problems, or major home repairs without forcing you back into debt to survive. The exact amount depends on your job security, health, and personal risk tolerance: government employees with great job security might be fine with three months of expenses, while commission-based salespeople or entrepreneurs should target six to twelve months given their income volatility.

Using credit cards responsibly means treating them as payment tools rather than borrowing instruments, only charging what you can pay off in full each month and never carrying a balance that accrues interest. For people who have struggled with credit card debt, the safest approach is often to eliminate credit cards entirely, switching to debit cards and cash to remove the temptation and psychological distance between spending and consequences. But if you're confident in your discipline and want the benefits of rewards programs and fraud protection, you can use credit cards carefully with strict rules: never charge something you couldn't buy with cash today, pay the full statement balance every month without exception, and immediately stop using cards if you ever carry a balance for any reason.

The cash envelope system, modernized for today's digital world, provides a powerful tool for controlling spending in categories where you tend to overspend or lose track. You allocate specific amounts of cash to different spending categories at the beginning of each month, putting physical bills in labeled envelopes for groceries, entertainment, dining out, and other variable expenses. When the envelope is empty, you stop spending in that category until next month, creating a hard physical limit that's impossible to ignore or rationalize away. This system is remarkably effective for people who struggle with overspending because it makes money tangible and spending immediately consequential in a way that swiping cards never does.

Modern variations replace physical cash with separate checking accounts or prepaid debit cards for each spending category, maintaining the psychological benefit of separated money while keeping the convenience of digital payments. You might have one checking account for fixed bills that's on autopay, one for groceries with a specific monthly deposit, one for discretionary spending, and one for saving and investing. The key principle remains: when an account hits zero, you stop spending in that category, enforcing discipline through systems rather than willpower.

Building a debt-free identity means shifting how you see yourself from someone who uses debt as a normal financial tool to someone who would never borrow money except for a carefully considered mortgage on an affordable home. This identity shift affects countless daily decisions that accumulate into your overall financial outcome. A person with a debt-using identity sees something they want and immediately thinks about whether they can afford the monthly payment, naturally gravitating toward financing options. A person with a debt-free identity sees something they want and immediately thinks about whether they can buy it with cash, naturally delaying purchases until they've saved the full amount.

Your financial identity is shaped by the people you spend time with, the content you consume, and the standards you hold yourself to regarding money. Surround yourself with debt-free people who view borrowing as slavery rather than opportunity, who save for purchases rather than financing them, and who prioritize financial freedom over immediate consumption. Consume content from financial voices that reinforce debt-free living and wealth building through ownership rather than leverage. Set standards for yourself that make debt unacceptable under virtually any circumstance, eliminating the internal negotiation that leads to rationalized borrowing.

The psychological freedom of debt elimination cannot be overstated and is worth far more than the interest dollars you save or the wealth you're now able to build. When you're debt-free, your entire monthly income belongs to you to deploy toward your priorities rather than being pre-committed to paying for things you bought in the past. You can take career risks like starting a business or switching fields without fear of missing debt payments. You can handle emergencies calmly rather than with panic about how you'll pay for them. You can make decisions based on what you actually want rather than what you can afford in monthly payments. This freedom transforms your entire life experience, reducing stress and anxiety while increasing options and possibilities.

Actionable Takeaways

The difference between understanding debt elimination principles and actually becoming debt-free is implementation, taking everything you've learned and translating it into specific actions executed consistently until the job is done. Most people who read about debt elimination feel motivated for a few days but never create concrete plans or systems, letting their initial enthusiasm fade without ever beginning the work. Commit right now to completing every action step this week, and you'll have done more than ninety-five percent of people who want to get out of debt but never actually do.

Debt Payoff Calculator:
Create a detailed debt elimination plan using either the avalanche or snowball method based on your personality and situation. List every debt with complete details including creditor name, total balance, interest rate, minimum payment, and current payment amount. Choose your strategy: avalanche for fastest payoff with least interest, snowball for quickest psychological wins, or hybrid for balanced approach. Calculate how much extra you can throw at debt beyond minimum payments through income increases and expense cuts. Use an online debt payoff calculator to project your exact debt-free date, seeing in specific terms when this nightmare ends if you stick to the plan.

Negotiation Scripts for Creditors:
Prepare specific scripts for negotiating lower interest rates with every credit card company, using the templates provided in this chapter and personalizing them for your situation. Schedule time this week to make calls to every single credit card company, asking for rate reductions and documenting results. For accounts where you're denied, note the date and try again in three to six months as circumstances and representatives change. Follow through on balance transfer threats if negotiations fail, actually moving debt to lower-rate cards rather than just talking about it.

Debt-Free Celebration Milestones:

Break your debt elimination journey into meaningful milestones that you'll celebrate along the way, creating motivation and acknowledging progress rather than waiting years for the final victory. Celebrate paying off your first debt, hitting twenty-five percent debt elimination, reaching the halfway point, and each subsequent debt that falls. These celebrations should be free or nearly free rather than expensive rewards that undermine your progress, but they should feel meaningful and special: a favorite home-cooked meal, a movie night with family, a day trip to somewhere beautiful, or any experience that acknowledges your sacrifice and progress.

Ninety-Day Debt Elimination Sprint Plan:

Create an intense ninety-day plan for maximum debt reduction, setting aggressive targets and specific actions you'll take to achieve them. Calculate exactly how much debt you'll eliminate in three months if you execute perfectly on all your plans: extra income from side hustle, savings from expense cuts, windfalls from selling possessions, and any other sources. Track your actual progress weekly, adjusting tactics as needed but maintaining intensity throughout the full ninety days. Many people find that three-month sprints are sustainable in ways that indefinite intensity is not, allowing you to go hard temporarily and then reassess before committing to another sprint.

The debt-free life is available to you regardless of how insurmountable your debt feels right now, regardless of how many times you've failed before, and regardless of what mistakes got you here. Thousands of people in worse situations than yours have eliminated six-figure debts and rebuilt their financial lives, not because they were special or lucky but because they decided the sacrifice was worth the freedom and they refused to quit when progress felt slow. You have everything you need to join them in debt freedom: a clear strategy, practical tools, and most importantly, the knowledge that your current situation is temporary unless you accept it as permanent.

Your journey to wealth begins not with investing or side businesses or real estate deals, but with this un glamorous work of eliminating debt and building your foundation. Every dollar you send to creditors right now is a dollar that will eventually be redirected toward building wealth instead of paying for the past, so this sacrifice isn't wasted effort but rather the prerequisite for everything else you want to achieve financially. The moment you make your final debt payment and realize you're truly free is one of the most powerful experiences of your life, worth every sacrifice you make to reach it.

4

Maximize Your Primary Income - Get Paid What You're Worth

Section 1: Becoming Invaluable at Your Job

Most people approach their jobs with a fundamentally flawed mindset, viewing employment as a transaction where they exchange the minimum acceptable effort for a paycheck rather than as an opportunity to become so valuable that employers compete to keep them and pay them more. This employee mindset keeps millions of talented people stuck at mediocre salaries while less skilled but more strategic colleagues leap ahead in compensation and career trajectory. The shift from employee mindset to invaluable contributor mindset represents one of the fastest paths to significant income increases without changing jobs or starting businesses, yet most people never make this shift because they don't understand the rules of the game they're playing.

Understanding what employers actually value, as opposed to what employees think they should value, is the first step toward becoming invaluable. Many people believe that working hard, showing up on time, and doing their assigned tasks competently should be enough to earn raises and promotions, and they feel frustrated and resentful when these things don't lead to the recognition they expect. The harsh reality is that basic competence is the minimum expectation, not an achievement worthy of premium compensation. What employers value and pay premium prices for is solving problems that matter to the business, generating revenue or saving costs, making leadership's lives easier, and demonstrating initiative that goes beyond job descriptions.

The ten-times employee mindset means approaching every task and project by asking yourself how you can deliver ten times more value than expected rather than just meeting the minimum requirements. This doesn't necessarily mean working ten times harder or longer hours, which is neither sustainable nor desirable; it means thinking strategically about what would create the most impact and focusing your energy there. If you're asked to create a report, don't just compile the requested data; analyze it for insights, identify patterns and opportunities, and present actionable recommendations that could generate revenue or prevent problems. If you're asked to solve a problem, don't just fix it once; create a system or process that prevents it from happening again and document it so others can use your solution.

This level of thinking and execution is rare enough that it immediately sets you apart from the majority of employees who do exactly what they're told and nothing more. When you consistently deliver beyond expectations and demonstrate the ability to think strategically rather than just executing tactically, you become the person management relies on for important projects, the one they can't imagine losing, and ultimately the one they'll pay premium salaries to retain. This positioning gives you enormous leverage in negotiations because your departure would create real pain and disruption rather than just requiring them to hire another warm body to fill a role.

Skills that command higher pay cluster around a few key categories that remain valuable across industries and economic conditions, and strategic investment in developing these skills creates compounding returns throughout your career. Revenue generation skills like sales, business development, marketing, and strategic partnerships are almost always among the highest paid because they directly contribute to the company's bottom line in measurable ways. If you can prove that your work generates more money than it costs to employ you, you have powerful leverage to demand higher compensation because you're profitable, not a cost center.

Problem-solving and analytical skills that allow you to tackle complex challenges, analyze data to extract insights, and develop innovative solutions to business problems are increasingly valuable in a world drowning in data but starving for insight. Companies will pay premium salaries to people who can look at information everyone has access to and see opportunities or risks that others miss, translating that analysis into strategies that create competitive advantage. This might mean learning advanced Excel and data analysis, studying business strategy and frameworks, or developing the ability to synthesize complex information into clear recommendations.

Leadership and management skills that enable you to multiply your impact through others rather than just doing individual contributor work eventually become essential for reaching the highest compensation levels in most careers. Individual contributors hit a ceiling on their earning potential because there are only so many hours in a day and only so much one person can accomplish alone, but leaders who can guide teams to achieve extraordinary results can command salaries multiples higher than top individual contributors. This doesn't mean you must become a manager if you don't want to, but understanding how to influence others, coordinate efforts, and create alignment around goals opens doors to higher compensation even in technical or specialist roles.

Technical expertise and deep specialized knowledge in your field creates value because you can accomplish in hours what would take others days or weeks, solving problems that others simply cannot solve regardless of effort or time investment. Becoming a recognized expert in a valuable niche, whether that's a specific software platform, regulatory domain, technical process, or market segment, allows you to command premium rates because your knowledge is scarce and valuable. This expertise takes years to develop, which is precisely why it's valuable; anyone could theoretically learn what you know, but very few people will actually put in the time and effort required.

Documenting your wins and contributions systematically throughout the year is essential for negotiation success because memory is unreliable and recency bias means that both you and your manager will disproportionately remember recent events while forgetting earlier accomplishments. Keep a running document where you record every significant achievement as it happens, including quantifiable results whenever possible: revenue generated, costs saved, problems solved, processes improved, initiatives launched, and recognition received. This documentation becomes your ammunition when asking for raises or defending your value during performance reviews.

The specifics matter enormously when documenting wins because vague claims about being a valuable employee are worthless compared to concrete examples with measurable results. Don't write "improved team efficiency" when you can write "redesigned the intake process, reducing average project kickoff time from two weeks to three days and allowing the team to handle forty percent more projects with the same headcount." Don't write "increased sales" when you can write "developed and executed outbound strategy that generated one point two million dollars in new annual recurring revenue, a thirty-five percent increase over prior year." These specific, quantified achievements tell a story that's impossible to dismiss or diminish.

Making yourself promotion-ready before the promotion is available means deliberately seeking out opportunities to demonstrate capabilities at the next level rather than waiting for permission to show what you can do. If you want to become a manager, start acting like one by mentoring junior team members, volunteering to lead projects, and thinking strategically about team effectiveness rather than just your individual tasks. If you want to move into a more senior technical role, start tackling the hardest technical problems, sharing knowledge through documentation and training, and consulting on projects outside your direct responsibilities.

This approach accelerates your career trajectory dramatically because when promotion opportunities arise, you're the obvious choice rather than an unproven gamble. You've already been operating at the higher level and delivering results, so promoting you is simply acknowledging reality rather than taking a risk on your potential. Meanwhile, your peers who were waiting for the promotion before stepping up their game remain stuck because they haven't proven they can handle the responsibility. The people who get promoted fastest are almost always those who started doing the job before they had the title, demonstrating value rather than just claiming they could provide it if given the chance.

Section 2: The Art of Negotiation

Salary negotiation represents one of the highest-return-on-time-invested activities in your entire financial life, potentially increasing your income by thousands or tens of thousands of dollars in exchange for a few hours of preparation and a thirty-minute conversation. Yet most people avoid negotiation entirely, accepting the first offer they receive out of fear, discomfort, or lack of knowledge about how the process works. This single failure costs them hundreds of thousands of dollars over their careers because every future raise and promotion builds on a base salary that was unnecessarily low from the start.

Understanding that negotiation is expected and welcomed by employers rather than seen as greedy or difficult is the first mindset shift required for successful negotiation. Employers expect candidates to negotiate, building room into their initial offers specifically for this purpose, and they actually respect candidates more for negotiating because it demonstrates confidence, business acumen, and an understanding of their own value. Hiring managers and HR professionals negotiate as part of their jobs; they're not offended or surprised when candidates do the same. In fact, accepting the first offer without discussion sometimes signals that you undervalue yourself or lack the negotiation skills required for the role.

Research and preparation form the foundation of successful negotiation because you cannot effectively negotiate from a position of ignorance about market rates, company budgets, or your own value. Before any negotiation, invest serious time in understanding what people in similar roles with similar experience at similar companies in your geographic market actually earn, not just what you want or what seems fair. Use resources like Glass door, Pay scale, Salary.com, and industry-specific salary surveys to gather data, but recognize that these sources often provide ranges so broad as to be nearly useless without additional context.

The most valuable salary information comes from actual conversations with people doing similar work at similar companies, which requires building a professional network and having the courage to ask direct questions about compensation. Reach out to people on LinkedIn who work in roles similar to what you're targeting, offering to buy them coffee or have a brief phone call to learn about their career path and the industry. Most people are surprisingly willing to share general compensation information when approached respectfully and when the request is framed as career research rather than nosiness. Even if they won't share their exact salary, they can usually tell you whether an offer you're considering is below, at, or above market rate.

Timing your negotiation request strategically dramatically impacts your likelihood of success because asking at the wrong moment, regardless of how deserving you are, often results in rejection that has nothing to do with your value. The best times to negotiate raises are after major wins when you've just delivered exceptional results and your value is most visible, during annual review cycles when budgets have been allocated for compensation adjustments, after taking on significantly more responsibility, and when you've received competing offers or approaches from recruiters that demonstrate external validation of your market value.

The worst times to negotiate are during company financial difficulties when budgets are frozen or being cut, right after your manager has fought unsuccessful battles to increase team compensation and has no political capital left, immediately after mistakes or failures before you've rebuilt credibility, and during periods of massive organizational change when no one wants to make commitments that might be undermined by restructuring. Reading the organizational context and timing your ask appropriately can mean the difference between a yes and a no for the exact same request and justification.

The actual negotiation conversation requires preparation of specific talking points and anticipated responses to common objections, transforming what could be an anxious improvisation into a structured discussion you can navigate confidently. Begin by expressing enthusiasm for the role or the company and genuine appreciation for the opportunity, establishing that you're negotiating from a position of wanting to make things work rather than adversarial dissatisfaction. Then present your case using specific accomplishments, market data, and a clear request for what you want, keeping emotion out of it and focusing purely on value delivered and market appropriateness.

Here's a script framework you can adapt for negotiating a raise: "I want to start by saying how much I've enjoyed contributing to the team this past year and how excited I am about the projects we have coming up. I've been thinking about my compensation and I'd like to discuss an adjustment that better reflects my contributions and the market rate for my role. Over the past year, I've accomplished X, Y, and Z, which generated measurable value including specific numbers and results. My research shows that similar roles in our market typically pay between this range and that range, and I'm currently at this level which is below that range. Based on my performance and market data, I'm requesting an increase to this specific number, which would bring me to the lower end of the market range for someone with my experience and results."

Notice several key elements in this script: it leads with positivity and enthusiasm rather than complaints or threats; it focuses on value delivered with specific examples rather than personal need or tenure; it incorporates market data to show the request is reasonable rather than arbitrary; and it makes a specific request for a specific number rather than asking vaguely for "more money" or "fair compensation." This structure works because it makes it easy for your manager to say yes by providing all the justification they'll need to advocate for your increase with their superiors or HR.

Handling objections and push back requires preparation for common responses and strategies for addressing them without becoming defensive or giving up too easily. If you're told "we don't have budget for that right now," ask when budget decisions are made and request to revisit the conversation at that time, while also asking what non-salary benefits might be available now such as additional vacation days, flexible work arrangements, professional development budget, or performance bonuses tied to specific achievements. If you're told "you need to prove yourself more first," ask for specific criteria and timelines, nailing down exactly what you need to accomplish and when you can expect to be reevaluated.

If you're told "that's just not how we do compensation here" or "everyone at your level makes the same," recognize that this might be true and you're hitting a genuine ceiling that requires changing companies rather than just negotiating better. Some organizations, particularly government agencies and highly bureaucratic companies, truly have rigid pay scales that leave little room for individual negotiation. In these cases, your best option is often to get promoted faster by making yourself indispensable and demonstrating readiness for the next level, or to look externally for companies that have more flexibility in compensation.

Negotiating with competing offers gives you maximum leverage but must be handled carefully to avoid burning bridges or coming across as mercenary. If you receive an external offer while employed and want to use it to negotiate a raise with your current employer, approach the conversation from a position of genuinely wanting to stay but needing the financial gap closed rather than wielding the offer as a threat. Share that you've been approached by another company and they've made an attractive offer, but you'd prefer to stay if you can reach an agreement on compensation that reflects your market value. Show the offer if asked, but don't issue ultimatums or set short deadlines unless you're genuinely prepared to leave.

Be aware that many companies have policies against counter-offering, and even when they do match external offers, they may view you as a flight risk and begin succession planning or limit your advancement opportunities. Some managers take counter-offer requests personally as a sign of disloyalty, particularly in smaller companies or tight-knit teams. This doesn't mean you shouldn't negotiate with competing offers, but it does mean you should be prepared to actually leave if the negotiation doesn't go well, rather than assuming you can always fall back on your current role with no consequences.

Section 3: Strategic Career Moves

Your career trajectory and earning potential are shaped not just by how you perform in your current role but by strategic decisions about when to stay with a company and when to move to a new opportunity. Many people approach career moves reactively, staying in roles until they're miserable or leaving impulsively when frustrated rather than making strategic decisions based on long-term financial and professional goals. Understanding the data and strategy behind job mobility can dramatically accelerate your income growth and career progression compared to the traditional path of company loyalty and waiting for annual raises.

The data on job hopping versus company loyalty is clear and somewhat surprising to people who came of age when lifetime employment at one company was the norm and the expected path to success. Multiple studies over the past decade show that people who change jobs every two to three years earn significantly more over their careers than people who stay at the same company for long periods, with differences ranging from twenty to fifty percent higher lifetime earnings for strategic job changers. This happens because external moves typically come with raises of ten to twenty percent or more, while internal raises average just three to five percent annually even for good performers.

The mathematics of this difference compound dramatically over a career: imagine two equally talented people starting at fifty thousand dollars annually. Person A stays with one company for ten years, receiving average raises of four percent per year, ending at about seventy-four thousand dollars after a decade. Person B changes companies three times during that same decade, receiving fifteen percent raises with each move and three percent raises in between, ending at approximately one hundred fifteen thousand dollars after ten years. The job hopper earned over five hundred thousand dollars more in cumulative income over the decade than the company loyalist, and this gap only widens over a full career as the higher base compounds through future raises and promotions.

However, job hopping has real costs and risks that must be factored into the decision beyond just the immediate salary increase. Frequent job changes can make you appear unstable or uncommitted on resumes, particularly if you're leaving roles after less than eighteen months or showing a clear pattern of short tenures. You lose out on longer-term projects and leadership opportunities that only come to people who stick around long enough to see initiatives through from start to finish. You never fully develop deep expertise or relationships at any organization, remaining somewhat perpetually junior despite years of experience. And you may miss out on equity grants, bonuses, or other long-term compensation that requires vesting periods to realize full value.

The optimal strategy for most people balances strategic external moves with meaningful tenure at companies where you're genuinely learning and advancing, creating a pattern that shows both progression and stability. Spend two to four years at each company during the early and middle parts of your career, long enough to deliver meaningful results and develop skills but not so long that your compensation falls significantly behind external market rates. Use external offers to accelerate raises at current employers when you genuinely want to stay, and leave for new opportunities when you've plateaued in learning or when compensation gaps become too wide to close through internal negotiation.

Geographic arbitrage through remote work opportunities has become one of the most powerful income maximization strategies since the COVID pandemic permanently normalized remote work for many knowledge workers. You can now potentially earn San Francisco or New York salaries while living in low cost-of-living areas, dramatically increasing your purchasing power and ability to save and invest. A one hundred twenty thousand dollar salary in San Francisco provides a similar lifestyle to seventy thousand in most mid-tier cities once you account for housing costs, taxes, and general cost of living, but that same one hundred twenty thousand salary in a low cost-of-living area provides wealth-building potential that's nearly impossible to match in expensive cities.

The key to successful geographic arbitrage is finding employers who pay based on role value rather than employee location, or who only adjust salaries partially for location differences. Some companies have embraced location-agnostic compensation, paying the same regardless of where you live because they're hiring for talent and impact rather than for filling seats in an office. Other companies use location tiers with meaningful but not proportional adjustments, perhaps paying twenty percent less for someone in a mid-tier city versus their headquarters city even though cost-of-living differences might be fifty percent or more. Both scenarios create opportunities for significant economic advantage through strategic relocation or remote work.

Be transparent with employers about your location and ensure you understand their policies, because attempting to hide your location or move without disclosure can result in termination or compensation claw backs if discovered. Some companies actively monitor employee locations through IP addresses, expense reports, or other means, and discovering undisclosed relocation is considered a trust violation that often results in firing. The opportunity for geographic arbitrage is significant enough that you don't need to be deceptive; simply target companies with favorable location policies rather than trying to game companies with strict location-based compensation.

Industry pivots that increase income often involve moving from industries with compressed salary ranges and limited growth potential to industries that pay premium prices for similar skills. If you're working in nonprofit, education, or government sectors and you have transferable skills, moving to technology, finance, or consulting can sometimes double your compensation for doing fundamentally similar work. A project manager in education might earn sixty thousand dollars annually, while a project manager at a tech company might earn one hundred thousand dollars or more for similar responsibilities and skill requirements.

This doesn't mean everyone should pile into the highest-paying industries regardless of fit or interest, because working in a field you hate for an extra twenty thousand dollars annually might not be worth the cost to your wellbeing and happiness. But if you're ambivalent about your current industry and you have skills that transfer to higher-paying sectors, making that pivot can dramatically accelerate your wealth-building timeline. The challenge is often convincing hiring managers that your skills translate when your background doesn't show obvious industry experience, which requires carefully crafting your resume and narrative to emphasize transferable skills and results rather than industry-specific tasks.

Section 4: Accelerating Your Career Growth

Long-term career success and increasing compensation require more than just doing your current job well; they require strategic thinking about how you're building a professional brand, developing valuable relationships, and creating opportunities that might not exist through formal channels. The difference between people who plateau at middle management or senior individual contributor roles and those who reach executive levels or start successful companies is often not talent or intelligence but rather their approach to career development as a long-term strategic project rather than a series of jobs.

Building a professional brand means establishing a reputation and visibility in your field that creates opportunities and leverage rather than always having to seek out and convince people of your value. Your professional brand is what people say about you when you're not in the room, the reputation that precedes you and influences whether you get called for opportunities or passed over for people with more visible accomplishments. In the early stages of your career, your brand might be primarily internal to your company, establishing yourself as the person who solves hard problems, ships projects on time, or brings energy and innovation to teams.

As your career progresses, building external brand visibility becomes increasingly important for accessing the best opportunities and commanding premium compensation. This might mean speaking at industry conferences about your expertise, writing articles or blog posts that demonstrate thought leadership, contributing to open-source projects or industry publications, serving on professional association boards, or building a significant following on professional social media platforms like LinkedIn or Twitter. These activities require time investment beyond your day job, but they create compounding returns through opportunities that seek you out rather than requiring you to constantly sell yourself.

Linked In optimization deserves special attention because it functions as your always-on professional advertisement, working on your behalf even when you're not actively job seeking. Most people treat Linked In as a static resume repository that they update once every few years, missing the enormous opportunity to use it as a dynamic platform for demonstrating expertise and building relationships. Optimize your profile with a professional photo, compelling headline that goes beyond your job title to describe the value you create, detailed experience sections that emphasize achievements over responsibilities, and regular sharing of content relevant to your industry that positions you as knowledgeable and engaged.

The activity matters as much as the profile itself because Linked In's algorithm rewards engagement, showing your content to more people when you consistently post, comment, and share. You don't need to become a Linked In influencer posting daily motivational content, but regularly sharing insights from your work, commenting thoughtfully on others' posts, and engaging with your network keeps you visible and top of mind. When recruiters search for candidates with your skills or when your network needs to refer someone for an opportunity, you're far more likely to be remembered and contacted if they've seen you actively participating rather than maintaining a dormant profile.

Networking that actually leads to opportunities requires moving beyond superficial connection collection to building genuine relationships with people who can help your career and whom you can help in return. The traditional networking advice of attending events and collecting business cards is largely useless in practice because brief interactions with strangers create no real connection or mutual obligation. Effective networking focuses on developing deeper relationships with a smaller number of strategic contacts through providing value, maintaining regular contact, and genuine interest in others' success rather than just what they can do for you.

Identify people whose career paths you admire or who work in roles or companies you're interested in, then find ways to provide value to them before asking for anything in return. This might mean sharing articles or resources relevant to their interests, making introductions to people who could help them, offering your expertise to help solve problems they're facing, or simply being a thoughtful sounding board for their challenges and ideas. Over time, these value-providing interactions build goodwill and relationship depth that make people genuinely want to help you when opportunities arise.

Mentorship and sponsorship represent different but equally important relationships for career acceleration, though many people confuse the two or only pursue mentorship while ignoring the even more critical sponsorship relationships. A mentor is someone who provides advice, perspective, and guidance based on their experience, helping you navigate challenges and make better decisions. Mentors are valuable and worth cultivating, but they're ultimately providing information rather than direct career advancement. A sponsor is someone with power and influence who actively advocates for you in rooms you're not in, recommending you for opportunities, defending your capabilities to skeptics, and using their political capital to advance your career.

Finding sponsors requires first becoming someone worth sponsoring by delivering exceptional results and demonstrating potential that makes betting on you a good investment for the sponsor's own reputation. You cannot directly ask someone to sponsor you the way you can ask for mentorship; sponsorship develops organically when influential people see your work and decide you're worth backing. However, you can create conditions favorable to sponsorship by ensuring your work is visible to senior leaders, volunteering for high-profile projects that showcase your abilities, and building relationships with powerful people who could advocate for you if they choose to invest in your success.

Side certifications and skills training can accelerate income growth when chosen strategically to fill specific skill gaps or meet clear market demands, but they can also be expensive wastes of time and money when pursued without clear strategy or market research. Before investing thousands of dollars and hundreds of hours in any certification or training program, validate that the credential actually increases earning potential in your target market rather than just sounding impressive. Talk to people in roles you want to move into and ask directly whether specific certifications helped them or would help someone trying to break into the field.

Technical certifications in cloud platforms like AWS, Azure, or Google Cloud, cybersecurity certifications like CISSP or CISM, project management certifications like PMP or agile certifications, and data science or analytics certifications can demonstrably increase earning potential when they address market demands for scarce skills. General business skills certifications or programs that don't teach specific in-demand technical skills often provide less clear ROI and should be approached more skeptically. An MBA from a top program can significantly boost earnings, but the same degree from a low-tier program might provide minimal benefit relative to its cost, making it crucial to evaluate specific programs rather than assuming all credentials in a category provide similar value.

Actionable Takeaways

Everything you've learned about maximizing your primary income through strategic career management and negotiation transforms your financial trajectory only when you actually implement it rather than just knowing it intellectually. The gap between people who dramatically increase their incomes and those who remain stuck at modest raises forever is action, the willingness to have uncomfortable conversations, make strategic moves, and invest in their own career development rather than passively accepting whatever their employer offers.

Salary Negotiation Script Templates:

Develop personalized scripts for three scenarios you're likely to face: negotiating a raise at your current job, negotiating a higher starting salary for a new role, and responding to low-ball offers. Start with the frameworks provided in this chapter and customize them for your specific situation, accomplishments, and market data. Practice these scripts out loud multiple times, ideally with a friend or partner playing the role of manager or recruiter, so the words feel natural and confident rather than rehearsed and stilted when you need to use them.

Career Growth Ninety-Day Plan:

Create a concrete ninety-day plan for becoming more valuable at your current job and positioning yourself for advancement or higher compensation. Identify three to five high-impact projects or initiatives you can lead or significantly contribute to that will deliver measurable results. Schedule time each week to document your achievements and update your accomplishments file with specific, quantified results. Set up informational interviews with three to five people in roles you're interested in moving toward, learning about their career paths and what skills were most important for advancement.

Skills Gap Analysis Worksheet:

Conduct an honest assessment of the skills required for the next level of your career compared to your current capabilities, identifying specific gaps that are holding you back from advancement or higher compensation. List the technical skills, leadership capabilities, industry knowledge, and professional credentials that people in your target role typically possess. Rate yourself honestly on each dimension and prioritize the gaps that are most critical to address, creating a learning plan with specific resources, timelines, and accountability measures for closing those gaps.

Linked In Optimization Checklist:

Transform your Linked In profile from a static resume into an active career development tool within the next week. Update your profile photo to a current, professional headshot. Rewrite your headline to emphasize the value you create rather than just listing your job title. Expand your experience sections to focus on achievements and results rather than responsibilities. Request recommendations from managers, colleagues, and clients who can speak to your capabilities. Begin posting or sharing content at least once per week related to your industry or expertise, commenting thoughtfully on others' posts to increase your visibility and engagement.

The income you earn from your primary employment is likely to remain your largest single income source for years to come as you build wealth, making optimization of this income stream one of the highest-leverage activities you can engage in. A ten thousand dollar raise earned through strategic negotiation and career management provides the same benefit as finding a side hustle that generates ten thousand dollars annually, but it requires far less ongoing time investment and becomes the base for all future raises and bonuses. Every dollar you add to your base salary this year compounds forward through your entire career, multiplying into hundreds of thousands of dollars of additional lifetime earnings.

Your value in the job market isn't fixed or determined by your employer; it's something you actively create through the skills you develop, the results you deliver, and the relationships you build. Taking control of this process rather than passively hoping for recognition transforms you from an employee waiting for raises to a professional strategically managing a valuable career asset. The discomfort of negotiating, the effort of building skills, and the risk of making strategic job moves are temporary prices you pay for permanently higher earning potential that accelerates every aspect of your wealth-building journey.

5

Multiple Income Streams - Never Rely on One Source

Section 1: The Millionaire's Secret

The vast majority of millionaires didn't build their wealth through a single income source, no matter how high that salary might have been. Studies consistently show that the average millionaire has seven different income streams, not because they're workaholics or because one source couldn't support their lifestyle, but because they understand a fundamental truth about wealth building that most people miss: diversified income provides both security and acceleration that single-source income can never match. When you rely entirely on one job for one hundred percent of your income, you're one layoff, one health crisis, or one company bankruptcy away from financial catastrophe regardless of how much you earn.

Understanding the difference between active and passive income fundamentally changes how you think about building wealth and allocating your time. Active income requires your direct participation and effort to generate; when you stop working, the income stops immediately. Your salary from employment is active income, as is revenue from freelancing, consulting, or any service business where you're trading time for money. Active income is essential and often forms the foundation of your wealth building, especially in the early years, but it's inherently limited by the hours in a day and your physical capacity to work.

Passive income, in contrast, continues flowing with minimal ongoing effort once the initial work of creating the income stream is complete. Rental income from properties you own, dividend payments from stocks, interest from bonds or savings, royalties from books or courses you created, and revenue from automated online businesses all represent passive income that works for you while you sleep, vacation, or focus on other priorities. The term passive is somewhat misleading because most passive income streams require significant upfront work to establish and periodic maintenance to sustain, but the key distinction is that your ongoing time investment is minimal relative to the income generated.

Building income streams while employed represents the optimal strategy for most people because it allows you to develop new revenue sources without the enormous risk of quitting your job and hoping your new venture succeeds before your savings run out. Your employment income provides stability, health insurance, and the financial cushion to experiment with income streams that might take months or years to become profitable. This approach requires working evenings and weekends for a period, sacrificing leisure time and social activities in service of future freedom, but it dramatically reduces the risk of entrepreneurship while maintaining the upside potential.

The psychological challenge of building side income while employed full-time is managing limited time and energy without burning out or sacrificing performance at your day job. Many people start side hustles with enthusiasm but quit within a few months because the sustained effort feels overwhelming when combined with full-time employment and family obligations. The key to sustainability is starting with manageable time commitments, perhaps five to ten hours weekly, and focusing on income streams that genuinely interest you or leverage existing skills so the work feels less like a second job and more like meaningful progress toward freedom.

Timeline expectations for new income streams must be realistic to avoid the disappointment and premature quitting that doom most side hustle attempts. Very few income streams generate significant money immediately; most require three to six months of consistent effort before producing even modest income, and twelve to twenty-four months before generating substantial revenue that meaningfully impacts your financial situation. Service-based businesses like freelancing or consulting can generate income faster, potentially within the first month if you have clients ready to go, but building a client base from scratch typically takes several months of marketing and networking.

Product-based income streams like online courses, digital downloads, or physical products usually take longer to become profitable because you must first create the product, build an audience or marketing channel, and refine your offering based on market feedback. Passive income streams like dividend investing or rental real estate take even longer because they require accumulating significant capital before the income becomes meaningful; one thousand dollars invested in dividend stocks generates perhaps thirty to forty dollars annually at typical yields, requiring hundreds of thousands invested before the passive income covers substantial expenses.

Understanding these timelines prevents the destructive cycle where people start income streams with unrealistic expectations, quit after a few weeks or months when they're not yet profitable, start something else with equal enthusiasm, quit again, and repeat this pattern for years without ever building anything substantial. Successful multiple income stream builders choose strategies aligned with their timeline expectations and commit to seeing them through the difficult early period when effort far exceeds income, trusting that consistency will eventually create the breakthrough they're working toward.

Section 2: Side Hustle Goldmine

Service-based side businesses represent the fastest path to generating additional income for most people because they require minimal startup capital, leverage skills you likely already possess, and can generate revenue immediately once you land your first clients. Instead of spending months building a product or audience before earning a dollar, you can start offering services today and potentially have paying clients this week if you have in-demand skills and know where to find people who need them. The trade-off is that service businesses are inherently active income, requiring your ongoing time and effort, but as starter income streams they're unmatched for speed to revenue.

Freelancing in your professional skill area is often the highest-leverage service business you can start because you're already competent at the work, you don't need to learn new skills before beginning, and you can often command rates similar to or higher than your hourly employment rate. If you're a graphic designer, accountant, writer, programmer, marketer, or possess any other skill that businesses need, you can begin freelancing by reaching out to your network, posting your services on platforms like Upwork or Fiverr, and directly contacting businesses that might need your expertise. Your first clients might come from former employers, colleagues, or friends who know your capabilities and can vouch for your quality.

The key to successful freelancing is positioning yourself strategically rather than competing purely on price with overseas workers or desperate freelancers who undervalue their time. Instead of offering generic services to anyone who will hire you, develop a specific niche and ideal client profile that allows you to charge premium rates because you deeply understand their needs and can deliver specialized value. A general freelance writer competing on price might earn twenty dollars per article; a freelance writer specializing in technical documentation for SaaS companies might earn three hundred dollars for similar effort because the latter has positioned themselves as a specialist solving a specific valuable problem.

Consulting takes freelancing to the next level by selling your expertise and advice rather than your execution labor, allowing you to command higher hourly rates while potentially delivering more value in less time. If you have deep knowledge in a specific domain through years of professional experience, you can consult with businesses facing challenges in that area, providing strategic guidance, training, or specialized expertise they can't get from generalists. A marketing consultant might charge two hundred to five hundred dollars per hour advising companies on strategy, while a marketing freelancer executing that strategy might earn fifty to one hundred dollars per hour doing the actual work.

The barrier to consulting is credibility; clients need to believe you have expertise worth paying premium rates for, which usually requires demonstrated track record, credentials, or results that prove your knowledge. If you're just starting your career, you probably can't position as a consultant yet because you haven't built the expertise or results that command consulting rates. But if you have ten-plus years in a field with measurable achievements, you have the raw material to package yourself as a consultant whose advice is worth significant money because following it helps clients avoid expensive mistakes or achieve better results than they could on their own.

Digital products like online courses, ebooks, templates, spreadsheets, design assets, or software tools represent a middle ground between pure service work and true passive income. Creating a digital product requires significant upfront time investment with no immediate return, but once created, it can generate sales with minimal ongoing effort beyond marketing and occasional updates. The economics are attractive: you create a product once and sell it hundreds or thousands of times, potentially earning far more per hour of invested effort than any service business could match, though only if the product actually sells at meaningful volume.

The challenge with digital products is that most fail to generate significant revenue because the creator built something they wanted to sell rather than something the market actually wants to buy at a price that makes the effort worthwhile. Before investing dozens or hundreds of hours creating a digital product, validate market demand by talking to potential customers, studying successful competing products, and potentially pre-selling the product before fully creating it. If you can't get people to commit to buying your course or ebook based on an outline and sample content, building the full product will likely result in something that sits on your hard drive generating zero income despite all your effort.

Local service businesses that scale like lawn care, house cleaning, pet sitting, handyman services, or mobile car detailing can generate substantial income if you're willing to do physical work and eventually build a team to multiply your efforts beyond what you can do personally. These businesses have the advantage of serving consistent local demand that won't disappear overnight, relatively low barriers to entry requiring more sweat equity than capital, and clear paths to scaling by hiring employees or contractors once you've proven the business model and have more clients than you can serve personally.

The income potential from local service businesses often surprises people who assume only tech startups or online businesses can generate serious money. A solo house cleaning business working full-time can generate fifty to seventy-five thousand dollars annually in many markets with minimal overhead; a cleaning business with a team of five to ten employees can generate several hundred thousand in annual revenue with proper management and marketing. The trade-off is that these businesses are often harder to automate or make passive than digital businesses, requiring ongoing management and problem-solving even after you hire others to do the actual service delivery.

Starting a local service business while employed requires careful time management and possibly sacrificing weekends or evenings for a period, but the financial returns can be substantial enough to create a genuine exit path from employment if that's your goal. Begin by offering services on weekends only, perhaps Saturdays to start, and gradually expand availability as you build a client base and confidence in the business. Many successful business owners spent a year or two running their business as a side project before having enough revenue and clients to quit their jobs and focus full-time on the venture.

Section 3: Passive Income Reality Check

The internet is filled with promises of passive income requiring minimal work to generate substantial wealth, creating dangerous misconceptions about how passive income actually works and leading thousands of people to waste time and money chasing unrealistic dreams. The reality of passive income is simultaneously less magical and more achievable than the hype suggests: it's not truly passive in most cases, it requires substantial upfront work or capital, and it takes years to build to meaningful levels, but it's absolutely possible to create income streams that generate money with minimal ongoing effort once established.

Rental income from property represents one of the most proven paths to genuine passive income, with millions of people building substantial wealth through real estate rentals over decades. The concept is straightforward: you purchase property, rent it to tenants at rates exceeding your costs, and collect the difference as income while building equity as the mortgage gets paid down and the property hopefully appreciates. A single rental property generating three hundred to five hundred dollars in monthly cash flow might not seem like much, but ten such properties generating four thousand dollars monthly in passive income can fund a comfortable lifestyle or accelerate wealth building dramatically.

The passive part of rental income is overstated because managing rental properties involves tenant screening, maintenance coordination, rent collection, lease renewals, and occasional major headaches like evictions or property damage that require significant time and stress. You can hire property managers to handle these tasks for typically eight to twelve percent of monthly rent, making the income more passive but reducing your cash flow accordingly. Even with professional management, you're still ultimately responsible for major decisions, capital investments, and ensuring the business runs profitably, so calling it completely passive stretches the truth.

Building a rental property portfolio requires either significant capital to purchase properties with cash or conventional mortgages, or creative financing strategies that allow you to acquire properties with minimal down payments through house hacking, FHA loans, seller financing, or partnerships. The barrier to entry is substantial, typically requiring at least twenty to twenty-five percent down for investment properties plus reserves for vacancies and repairs, meaning your first rental property might require thirty to fifty thousand dollars in capital depending on the property value in your market. This is why rental income typically comes later in wealth building rather than as a starting strategy for people still eliminating debt and building emergency funds.

Dividend-paying stocks provide another avenue to passive income that's more accessible to beginners because you can start with small amounts and build gradually, though generating meaningful income requires substantial invested capital. Companies that pay dividends distribute a portion of their profits to shareholders quarterly, providing income in addition to potential stock price appreciation. A stock yielding three percent annually means that one hundred thousand dollars invested generates three thousand dollars in annual dividend income, which is nice but not life-changing for most people.

The passive income from dividends is genuinely passive once you've invested the money; you simply hold the stocks and receive quarterly payments without any work required beyond occasionally reviewing your portfolio to ensure the investments remain sound. The challenge is that building dividend income to substantial levels requires investing hundreds of thousands or millions of dollars, which takes decades for most people saving and investing from employment income. Someone investing five hundred dollars monthly in dividend stocks averaging three percent yields takes about fifteen years to build one hundred thousand dollars in principal, generating just three thousand dollars annually in dividends after all that time and effort.

Digital assets like blogs, YouTube channels, podcasts, or online courses can generate passive income through advertising, sponsorships, affiliate marketing, or product sales, but the passive nature only kicks in after months or years of intensive content creation builds an audience large enough to generate meaningful revenue. A blog generating five thousand dollars monthly in passive income sounds amazing until you learn that it took the creator three years of publishing multiple posts per week and building backlinks before the traffic and revenue reached that level, representing hundreds of hours of unpaid work before the income materialized.

The harsh reality of digital asset passive income is that most attempts fail to ever generate significant money because building an audience in today's saturated online environment is extraordinarily difficult unless you have unique expertise, exceptional content quality, strategic marketing savvy, or substantial luck. For every successful blogger or YouTuber earning meaningful passive income, thousands quit after months of effort generated single-digit dollars in Ad Sense revenue or affiliate commissions. This doesn't mean you shouldn't try if you're genuinely passionate about creating content and have something valuable to share, but approach it with realistic expectations about the effort required and the probability of meaningful financial success.

Royalties and licensing from creative or intellectual property represent another passive income stream available primarily to people who create copyright able or patent able work that has ongoing commercial value. Authors earn royalties from book sales, musicians earn royalties from streaming and licensing, inventors earn royalties from patented products they license to manufacturers, and photographers or designers earn passive income from stock photography or design asset libraries. Once the work is created and distributed through appropriate channels, it can generate income for years or decades with minimal ongoing effort.

The barrier to royalty income is creating something of sufficient quality and market appeal that people are willing to pay for it at volume, which is far harder than it sounds. Self-publishing a book is easy; writing a book that sells thousands of copies and generates meaningful royalty income requires exceptional writing, strategic marketing, and either lucky timing or deep understanding of what audiences want. Most books sell fewer than two hundred copies total; most music uploaded to streaming platforms earns dollars rather than thousands; most stock photos never sell. The few creators who build substantial passive royalty income usually have multiple products and years of consistent creation building their catalog and audience.

The work behind "passive" income is the critical truth that get-rich-quick promoters conveniently omit when selling courses on passive income creation. Every passive income stream shown in this section required either substantial upfront capital that took years to accumulate, intensive initial effort creating assets that might or might not generate returns, ongoing maintenance and management that isn't truly passive, or some combination of all three. Passive income is achievable and genuinely powerful for wealth building, but it's not easy, quick, or effortless, which is why most people never build it to meaningful levels despite knowing it's important.

Section 4: Scaling from Side Income to Main Income

The transition from side income generating a few hundred dollars monthly to main income replacing your employment salary and supporting your lifestyle represents a critical inflection point that many people dream about but few successfully navigate. The difference between eternal side hustlers who never escape their day jobs and successful entrepreneurs who build businesses replacing and eventually exceeding their employment income is usually not talent or luck but strategic thinking about when and how to make the leap. Scaling too early before your side income is stable and sufficient destroys businesses and forces defeated entrepreneurs back to employment; scaling too late or never at all traps people in exhausting double workloads of employment plus side business indefinitely.

Knowing when it's time to scale from side to main income requires evaluating multiple factors beyond just the raw monthly revenue your side business generates. First, your side income should consistently exceed your monthly expenses for at least three to six months, demonstrating that it's not a lucky spike but sustainable revenue that can support your life. Second, you should have six to twelve months of expenses saved as a runway buffer because transitioning to self-employment almost always involves some income dip or volatility that your savings must cover. Third, you should have clear visibility into your pipeline or future revenue sources, knowing where the next few months of income will come from rather than just hoping clients or customers continue appearing magically.

Fourth, you should have systems and processes documented so your business can function even when you're sick, on vacation, or dealing with personal emergencies rather than completely dependent on your daily personal involvement. Fifth, your business should have growth potential beyond what you can achieve working evenings and weekends, meaning that dedicating full-time hours would meaningfully increase revenue rather than just giving you more free time with similar income. If these conditions aren't met, you're not ready to make side income your main income regardless of how frustrated you are with employment or how exciting full-time entrepreneurship sounds.

The conservative approach to transitioning from employment to self-employment involves reducing your employment to part-time while scaling your business, giving you a income safety net and benefits while dedicating more hours to growing your venture. Some employers allow valued employees to reduce to three or four days weekly, providing eighty percent of salary while freeing up one or two days for business building. This arrangement is ideal if you can negotiate it because it dramatically reduces risk while accelerating your business growth through additional focused time. The downside is that many employers won't accommodate part-time arrangements for professional roles, forcing you to choose between full-time employment or complete independence.

The aggressive approach involves quitting employment once your side income reaches fifty to seventy-five percent of your expenses and you have substantial savings, betting that the additional time and focus will allow you to quickly scale to full expense coverage and beyond. This approach accelerates your transition and forces intensity that often produces faster growth than cautious part-time entrepreneurship, but it's obviously higher risk and unsuitable for people with dependents, high fixed expenses, low risk tolerance, or businesses that might not scale predictably with additional time investment. Young, single people with low expenses and high savings can often afford this aggressive approach; parents with mortgages and one income usually cannot.

Systems and automation become critical as you scale because the tactics that worked for generating a few thousand dollars monthly in side income often don't scale to generating ten or twenty thousand monthly without burning you out or requiring impossible working hours. When you were serving five clients, you could personally handle every email, every deliverable, and every customer service issue; when you're serving fifty clients, that same approach means working eighty-hour weeks and never sleeping. Systematizing your business means documenting processes, creating templates and automation wherever possible, and potentially hiring contractors or employees to handle tasks that don't require your specific expertise.

Start systematizing even while your business is small, creating documentation and process frameworks that will scale with you rather than waiting until you're drowning in operational chaos to finally admit you need systems. Document how you onboard clients, fulfill your service or deliver your product, handle customer service issues, manage your finances and invoicing, and market to attract new customers. Initially these documents serve as reference to ensure consistency; eventually they become training materials for people you hire to help you scale. The business owners who successfully scale are almost always those who think like system builders rather than individual contributors, creating leveraged operations rather than just trading their time for money at larger scale.

Hiring your first help represents a pivotal moment that separates solo-preneurs working hard for modest income from business owners building something that can grow beyond their personal capacity. Many people resist hiring for far too long out of fear of the commitment, concern about finding trustworthy help, or reluctance to share the profits, staying trapped in a business that can never grow beyond what one person can accomplish personally. Others hire too quickly before they have systems and consistent revenue, creating fixed costs that destroy their cash flow and force them back to solo operation or out of business entirely.

The right time to hire is when you have more demand than you can personally handle, established systems for delivering quality work consistently, and consistent revenue that would easily cover the help's cost plus margin. Start with contractors rather than employees if possible because they provide flexibility without the legal complexities and overhead of employment, allowing you to scale up and down with demand. Your first hire should handle tasks that are time-consuming but don't require your specific expertise, freeing you to focus on high-value activities only you can do like strategy, business development, and high-level client relationships.

The transition plan from employee to entrepreneur should be detailed and specific rather than a vague hope that things will work out, mapping the key milestones you must hit and the financial metrics that will determine whether you're on track or need to reassess. Write down your target monthly revenue at three months, six months, and twelve months post-transition, along with the key client acquisitions or product launches required to hit those targets. Identify your monthly expense minimum and runway duration, knowing exactly how long you can sustain yourself if revenue doesn't meet projections. Establish clear decision points where you'll evaluate whether the business is working or whether you need to return to employment before depleting your savings completely.

This planning might seem pessimistic or lacking in entrepreneurial faith, but it's actually the mark of mature business thinking that separates successful entrepreneurs from broke dreamers. Having clear metrics and decision points prevents you from floating in denial while your business slowly fails and your savings dwindle, forcing either course corrections or tactical retreat before you've lost everything. Many successful entrepreneurs tried multiple business ideas before finding one that worked, but they were able to try multiple times because they didn't bet everything on attempt number one and retained the resources to try again after intelligent failures.

Actionable Takeaways

The gap between people who successfully build multiple income streams and those who remain stuck with single-source income forever is almost never knowledge or opportunity; it's action, the willingness to start before you feel completely ready and maintain consistency through the inevitable difficult early period when effort far exceeds results. Everything you've learned in this chapter provides the framework and strategy, but implementation creates the actual income that transforms your financial situation and accelerates your journey to wealth.

Income Stream Assessment Matrix:

Create a comprehensive assessment of potential income streams based on your skills, resources, interests, and constraints, evaluating each opportunity against specific criteria before committing time and energy. List ten to twenty possible income streams you could potentially pursue, ranging from freelancing in your professional skills to product creation to local services to investing-based passive income. Rate each option on time to first dollar of revenue, income potential at one year, required startup capital, alignment with existing skills, personal interest and sustainability, and scalability potential. This matrix helps you choose strategically rather than impulsively chasing whatever sounds exciting or easy in the moment.

Side Hustle Idea Generator:

Use this structured approach to generate viable side hustle ideas based on your unique situation rather than copying generic suggestions that might not fit you. First, list your professional skills that businesses or individuals might pay for outside your employment. Second, list your hobbies or interests where you have above-average knowledge or capability. Third, list problems you've solved or systems you've built that others struggle with. Fourth, list local service needs in your area that seem underserved or poorly served. Fifth, list products you wish existed or existing products you could improve or serve a niche better. From these lists, identify the three to five ideas that combine your skills, market demand, and genuine interest, making them candidates for serious pursuit.

Passive Income Calculator:

Calculate how much passive income you could realistically build over five and ten years through different strategies, using conservative assumptions about returns and your ability to invest. For dividend investing, assume you invest a specific monthly amount and earn three to four percent yields, calculating total invested and annual passive income at five and ten years. For rental real estate, assume you purchase one property every two to three years at specific cash flow amounts, calculating total monthly passive income from multiple properties over time. For digital products or content creation, assume extremely conservative revenue growth since most attempts fail, but model what success could look like if you're in the lucky minority who persevere and succeed.

Six-Month Side Hustle Launch Plan:

Create a detailed week-by-week plan for launching your chosen side income stream over the next six months, breaking the overwhelming project into specific actionable tasks that you can accomplish in your available time. Month one focuses on validation and preparation: researching the market, identifying potential customers, creating your minimum viable offer, and establishing basic systems. Month two focuses on launch and first customers: announcing your services, reaching out to your network, creating marketing materials, and landing your first paying clients or customers. Months three through six focus on refinement and growth: improving your offering based on feedback, systematizing delivery, increasing marketing efforts, and scaling to your target monthly income.

Building multiple income streams is not about working yourself to death juggling five different hustles simultaneously; it's about strategically developing complementary revenue sources over time that together create security, acceleration, and eventually the option for financial independence. Your employment income might remain your largest source for years while you build others, and that's perfectly fine because the goal is not to replace it quickly but to ensure you're not trapped in complete dependence on a single source that could disappear with one conversation with HR.

The most successful wealthy people almost universally have diversified income rather than dependence on single sources, not because any individual stream is small but because they understand that resilience and opportunity come from having multiple bets placed rather than everything riding on one outcome. Start building your second income stream now, before you desperately need it, and commit to seeing it through the difficult early period when results feel disproportionately small compared to effort. The compound effect works on income streams just like it works on investments; the streams you start today will be paying dividends five and ten years from now when newer entrepreneurs are just beginning their journeys.

6

Entrepreneurship - Building Wealth Through Business

Section 1: The Entrepreneurial Wealth Advantage

Entrepreneurship represents the fastest path to significant wealth for people without inherited money or exceptional professional credentials, which is why Forbes lists of billionaires contain overwhelmingly more business founders than employees regardless of industry or position. The mathematics of business ownership create wealth-building advantages that employment fundamentally cannot match, allowing entrepreneurs who succeed to accumulate in years what employees might take decades to build through savings and investing alone. Understanding these structural advantages explains why so many people are drawn to entrepreneurship despite its risks and challenges, and why building or buying a business deserves serious consideration in any comprehensive wealth-building strategy.

The wealth creation potential of successful businesses dwarfs what's possible through employment because businesses create equity value beyond just the income they generate for owners. An employee earning two hundred thousand dollars annually who saves and invests aggressively might build two to three million dollars in net worth over a twenty-five year career through compound investment returns. A business owner whose company generates two hundred thousand dollars in annual profit might build that same personal net worth in five to ten years through a combination of the business's cash flow and the equity value of the business itself, which could be worth two to five times annual profit depending on the industry and business model.

This equity value represents the biggest wealth difference between business ownership and employment because while employees can save and invest their income, business owners can eventually sell their businesses for multiples of annual profit, creating liquidity events that can instantly transform their financial situations. A software business generating five hundred thousand dollars in annual profit might sell for two to four million dollars; a manufacturing business with similar profits might sell for one to two million; even service businesses that are harder to sell can often fetch one to two times annual profit from the right buyer. That liquidity event creates wealth that would take employees decades to accumulate through saving and investing.

Tax advantages of business ownership provide another structural benefit that employees cannot access regardless of how much they earn or how sophisticated their tax planning becomes. Business owners can deduct ordinary and necessary business expenses before calculating taxable income, including home office expenses, vehicle costs for business use, travel and meals related to business activities, equipment and technology purchases, professional development and education, and countless other expenses that employees pay with after-tax dollars. These deductions aren't cheating or aggressive tax avoidance; they're legitimate recognition that business expenses reduce actual profit and shouldn't be taxed as income.

The tax savings compound over time into substantial wealth-building advantages that most people dramatically underestimate until they experience them firsthand. Consider two people each generating one hundred fifty thousand dollars annually, one as an employee and one as a business owner. The employee pays income tax on the full one hundred fifty thousand minus limited deductions like retirement contributions and mortgage interest, perhaps paying forty thousand in federal and state taxes and taking home one hundred ten thousand. The business owner with similar revenue might have fifty thousand in legitimate business deductions for office space, equipment, travel, contractors, software, and other expenses, paying tax on just one hundred thousand of income and taking home perhaps eighty-five thousand after taxes but having benefited from fifty thousand in expenses that would cost an employee sixty-five thousand or more after-tax dollars to obtain.

Building equity through business ownership means that every dollar of profit you retain in the business increases its value and your net worth, creating compounding wealth accumulation that happens faster than most people realize. Unlike employment where your net worth increases only through saving income and investing it elsewhere, business ownership allows you to build wealth through retained earnings that increase both the business's capacity to generate future profit and its value if you eventually sell. A business that starts generating fifty thousand in annual profit and retains most of that cash to fund growth might be worth one hundred thousand in year one, but worth five hundred thousand in year five if profit has grown to two hundred thousand annually through reinvestment of those retained earnings.

This equity accumulation happens alongside the income you're taking from the business for living expenses, meaning successful business owners are often building wealth through multiple mechanisms simultaneously: taking distributions for current lifestyle funding, retaining earnings that grow business value, and creating intellectual property or systems that have value independent of ongoing revenue. The combination of these wealth-building mechanisms working together explains why business ownership can create wealth so much faster than employment even when the raw income numbers might be similar in successful cases.

Scalability and leverage represent the final major advantage of business ownership over employment, creating the possibility for your income to increase dramatically without proportional increases in your time investment once proper systems are in place. An employee's income is fundamentally limited by hours available to work and the maximum salary their employer will pay for their role; doubling your income as an employee usually means either finding a much higher-paying job or working twice as many hours, neither of which is easily achievable. A business owner can double revenue through strategic marketing, improved systems, hiring additional staff, or product improvements without necessarily doubling their personal work hours.

This scalability means that business ownership has essentially unlimited income potential for people who succeed at building systematized, growing enterprises, while employment has relatively fixed ceilings regardless of effort or skill. The highest-paid employees in most companies might earn five to ten times what average employees make, a significant spread but ultimately bounded by organizational pay structures and market rates. The most successful business owners might earn one hundred or one thousand times what struggling business owners make, with essentially no ceiling beyond market size and their ability to capture and serve it. This unlimited upside attracts ambitious people to entrepreneurship despite the very real possibility of earning nothing or losing money if the business fails.

Section 2: Finding Your Profitable Business Idea

Most aspiring entrepreneurs waste months or years waiting for the perfect business idea to strike them like lightning, convinced that successful businesses start with brilliant inspiration rather than systematic identification of market problems and customer needs. The reality is that most successful businesses started with fairly ordinary ideas executed well, solving real problems for paying customers rather than pursuing the founder's passion or building something technologically impressive but commercially unviable. Understanding how to identify genuinely profitable business ideas rather than just interesting concepts separates successful entrepreneurs from the majority who burn through savings and eventually give up after pursuing ideas that were never going to work.

The problem-solving approach to business ideas starts with identifying genuine frustrations or inefficiencies that people or businesses experience regularly and would pay money to solve or improve. Instead of asking "what business should I start" or "what am I passionate about," start by observing where people are struggling, complaining, or wasting time and money on inadequate solutions. Every successful business exists because it solves some problem better, faster, cheaper, or more conveniently than the alternatives including doing nothing, which is why businesses that don't solve real problems fail even when the founders work hard and the product or service is well-executed.

Talk to potential customers before building anything, asking about their biggest frustrations and challenges in areas where you might have expertise or interest, listening carefully for problems they'd pay money to solve. These conversations often reveal that the problems you assumed people had aren't actually painful enough to warrant spending money, while other problems you hadn't considered are causing significant frustration and expense. A software developer might assume people want a more feature-rich tool when customers actually want something simpler and easier to use; a service provider might assume price is the main concern when customers actually care more about reliability and communication.

The pattern you're looking for is people expressing frustration about current solutions and actively seeking alternatives, demonstrating that they have a genuine problem rather than just a mild preference. Someone who says "yeah, it would be nice if that was better" probably won't become a paying customer; someone who says "I waste hours every week dealing with this and I've tried three different solutions but they all have major issues" is signaling a real problem they'd likely pay to solve. Pay attention to problems where people have already spent money trying to solve them but remain dissatisfied, because this proves both willingness to pay and inadequacy of current solutions.

Market validation before you launch means testing whether people will actually give you money for your proposed solution before you invest months building a complete product or business. Many entrepreneurs build elaborate products or services that no one wants to buy, discovering only after wasting enormous time and money that their idea had no real market demand. Smart entrepreneurs validate demand with minimal investment through techniques like pre-selling, landing pages measuring interest, service offerings to early customers before building full infrastructure, or minimum viable products that test core value proposition with minimal features.

Pre-selling means selling your product or service before it fully exists, using the revenue and customer commitments to validate demand and fund development. This might mean offering consulting services before building a course, selling custom work before creating productized offerings, or taking pre-orders with clear timelines before manufacturing products. Pre-selling is the ultimate validation because people are giving you actual money rather than just expressing interest or taking a free sample, proving that your value proposition resonates strongly enough to overcome skepticism about buying something that doesn't yet exist. The customers who believe in your vision enough to pre-buy become your best early evangelists and provide crucial feedback for shaping your offering.

Landing pages measuring interest provide cheaper validation for ideas where pre-selling isn't feasible or feels premature, testing whether people are interested enough to click and provide their email before you build anything substantial. Create a simple web page describing your proposed product or service and its benefits, offering early access or special pricing to people who provide their email address, then drive traffic through paid ads, social media, or your network and measure what percentage of visitors convert. If you can't get even one to three percent of targeted visitors to give you their email for early access to something you described compellingly, you probably won't be able to convert them to paying customers later when you actually have something to sell.

Low-cost business models that let you start with minimal capital reduce financial risk and allow you to test ideas without betting everything on unproven concepts. Service businesses where you're selling your time and expertise require almost no startup capital beyond perhaps a website and some basic tools, making them ideal first businesses for people without significant savings. Digital products have similarly low startup costs since creating and distributing digital content costs nearly nothing compared to physical products requiring inventory, manufacturing, and logistics. Even some physical product businesses can start with minimal capital through drop shipping models where you never hold inventory, or through small initial production runs that test market demand before committing to large inventory purchases.

The best first business for most people is one that can generate revenue quickly with minimal upfront investment, allowing you to prove the concept and generate cash flow before expanding. This might not be the business that will make you wealthy long-term, but it gets you into entrepreneurship with manageable risk while teaching you crucial lessons about finding customers, delivering value, and running operations. Many successful entrepreneurs started with simple service businesses that funded their learning and eventual transition to more scalable product businesses that created real wealth, rather than trying to build their ultimate dream business from day one with no experience or capital.

Service versus product businesses present fundamentally different trade-offs in terms of startup requirements, scalability, and wealth-building potential that you must understand before choosing which path to pursue. Service businesses are easier to start because they require minimal capital, can generate revenue immediately once you land clients, and leverage skills you likely already have from professional experience. The downside is that service businesses are inherently limited by your available time and are difficult to sell unless you build a firm with systems and a team that can operate without you.

Product businesses, whether physical products or software, require more upfront investment and usually take longer to generate revenue, but they offer better scalability and equity value because they're not dependent on your personal time and effort to deliver value. A software product can serve one customer or ten thousand customers with similar marginal costs, while a service business must add people or hours to serve more clients. This scalability means product businesses can grow faster and build more valuable equity than most service businesses, but only if you can successfully create a product people actually want to buy and figure out how to market and sell it at scale.

Many entrepreneurs wisely start with service businesses to generate immediate income and learn about their market, then transition to product businesses once they understand customer needs deeply and have capital to invest in product development. A consultant might sell custom strategy work for two years while observing patterns in client problems, then create a software tool or training program that solves the most common problems at scale. A freelance designer might do client work initially, then develop templates or design systems they can sell repeatedly. This progression lets you de-risk entrepreneurship by generating income while learning, rather than betting everything on a product that might not find a market.

Section 3: Starting Lean and Smart

The lean startup methodology has transformed how smart entrepreneurs approach new ventures, replacing the traditional approach of extensive planning and upfront investment with rapid experimentation and validation that minimizes wasted time and money. Traditional business planning assumed you could predict the future through careful analysis and planning, leading entrepreneurs to spend months writing detailed business plans and raising capital before discovering that customers didn't actually want what they built. Lean startup recognizes that most initial assumptions are wrong and focuses on testing those assumptions as quickly and cheaply as possible, learning from real market feedback rather than hypothetical plans.

Bootstrap versus funding represents a crucial strategic decision that shapes every aspect of how you build your business and what outcomes you can realistically expect. Bootstrapping means funding the business yourself through personal savings, revenue from early customers, or other sources that don't involve giving up equity or taking on significant debt. This approach maintains complete ownership and control while forcing financial discipline and focus on revenue generation, but it limits how fast you can grow and what opportunities you can pursue compared to funded competitors who can outspend you on talent, marketing, and product development.

Outside funding through angel investors, venture capital, or even friends and family provides capital to hire faster, market more aggressively, and potentially dominate a market before competition can catch up, but it means giving up ownership stakes and often significant control over strategic decisions. Venture-backed companies must pursue aggressive growth targets to justify their valuations and provide returns to investors, eliminating the option to build profitable lifestyle businesses that generate comfortable income but don't have explosive growth potential. This pressure leads many funded startups to swing for massive outcomes and either succeed spectacularly or fail completely, while bootstrapped businesses can succeed at smaller scales that still create substantial wealth for founders.

For most people reading this book, bootstrapping makes more sense than pursuing funding because it allows you to build wealth through profitable businesses that you fully own rather than gambling on long-shot huge exits that reward investors more than founders. The wealth advantage of owning one hundred percent of a business generating five hundred thousand in annual profit dramatically outweighs owning twenty percent of a business generating five million in revenue but burning through investor capital trying to grow to fifty million. Bootstrapped businesses that reach profitability can sustain indefinitely and compound wealth through retained earnings and owner distributions, while funded businesses must eventually exit through acquisition or IPO or they fail regardless of profitability.

The minimum viable product approach means building and launching the simplest possible version of your product or service that delivers core value to early customers, then improving it based on real feedback rather than your assumptions about what customers want. Your MVP should be almost embarrassingly basic, containing only the essential features needed to solve the core problem and nothing else, allowing you to launch in weeks or months rather than years. This feels uncomfortable for perfectionist entrepreneurs who want to launch with polished, feature-complete products, but it's crucial for avoiding the common failure mode of spending years building something nobody wants.

Testing before fully committing means maintaining your day job and building your business as a side project until revenue and validation clearly justify making it your full focus and primary income source. This approach frustrates people who want to dive in completely and feel like real entrepreneurs, but it dramatically reduces financial risk and prevents the scenario where you quit your job with no safety net and desperately try to make the business work while your savings drain and stress compounds. The vast majority of successful businesses started as side projects that proved their viability before founders committed fully, not because those founders lacked courage but because they were smart about managing risk.

Build your business on nights and weekends for six months to a year, using that time to validate that customers will actually pay for what you're offering and that you can deliver profitably at small scale before betting your financial security on scaling up. This testing period teaches you invaluable lessons about your market, your offering, and your own capability and interest in running this particular business, insights you cannot get from planning and research alone. Many people discover during this testing period that they don't actually enjoy the business they thought would be perfect, or that the market isn't as ready as they assumed, saving themselves from the disaster of quitting their jobs to pursue something that wouldn't have worked anyway.

Side business while keeping your job requires discipline and time management that many people struggle with, but it's absolutely achievable if you're serious about building something rather than just dabbling. Wake up an hour earlier and work on your business before your day job, use your lunch break for business development calls or marketing tasks, spend evenings and weekends on product development or service delivery, and eliminate time-wasting activities that don't serve your goals. This schedule is exhausting and unsustainable forever, but you don't need to maintain it forever; you just need to sustain it long enough to prove your business works and build it to the point where transitioning makes financial sense.

The beauty of this approach is that failure costs you only time and perhaps a few thousand dollars in small expenses, not your savings, your family's security, or years of your career. If the business doesn't work, you still have your job and income to fall back on while you try a different idea or decide entrepreneurship isn't for you. This acceptable downside combined with the unlimited upside of business success makes starting as a side project the most sensible path for anyone who can't afford to be unemployed while figuring out if their idea works.

Section 4: Building a Business That Runs Without You

The difference between owning a job and owning a business is whether the enterprise can function and generate profit without your constant personal involvement, a distinction that determines both your quality of life as an owner and the value of the business if you ever want to sell it. Many entrepreneurs build businesses that completely depend on them personally, creating golden handcuffs where they're trapped working harder than any employee and unable to take vacations or even sick days without the business grinding to a halt. These owner-dependent businesses have minimal sellable value because they're buying your labor rather than a true business asset that generates profit independent of any particular person.

Systems and standard operating procedures represent the foundation of a business that runs without you, documenting how every important task and process should be completed so that anyone with proper training can execute them successfully. Most entrepreneurs resist creating SOPs because it feels bureaucratic and time-consuming when they could be working on revenue-generating activities, but this short-term thinking keeps them trapped in operational work forever rather than freed to focus on strategy and growth. The time you invest documenting your processes is repaid many times over through faster employee training, consistent quality, and the ability to delegate work without constant oversight.

Start documenting systems before you feel ready or have employees to use them, creating SOPs as you develop processes rather than trying to reconstruct them from memory later when you're desperate to hire help. Every time you complete an important task, spend ten extra minutes writing down the steps you took and any key decisions or considerations someone else would need to know. These initial rough drafts don't need to be perfect; they just need to capture the essential process so you have a starting point to refine as you repeat the task and learn what works. Over months or years, you'll build a comprehensive operations manual that contains the institutional knowledge of how your business actually works rather than that knowledge existing only in your head.

The return on investment in systems development is difficult to calculate precisely but undeniably massive when you consider the alternative of remaining trapped in every operational detail of your business forever. Documented systems allow you to delegate confidently, hire people more easily, scale operations without proportionally scaling chaos, take vacations without anxiety about things falling apart, and eventually sell your business for significant multiples of what an owner-dependent business would fetch. A business with comprehensive documented systems might sell for three to five times annual profit, while a business completely dependent on the owner might sell for one times annual profit or not at all if buyers can't see how it would function without you.

Hiring and team building transform your business from a solopreneurial grind into a genuine company with the leverage to grow beyond your personal capacity, but hiring wrong or too fast destroys more businesses than under-hiring ever did. The first few hires are crucial because they establish the culture and capabilities that will shape all future growth, and early hiring mistakes compound through their impact on customers, other employees, and your own stress levels. Hire too slow and you miss opportunities while burning yourself out trying to do everything personally; hire too fast and you create fixed costs that drain cash flow while potentially bringing on people who hurt more than help.

Your first hire should handle tasks that are time-consuming but don't require your specific expertise, freeing your time to focus on activities only you can do like strategy, key customer relationships, and business development. For service businesses, this might be an assistant who handles scheduling, invoicing, and basic customer service. For product businesses, it might be someone handling fulfillment, customer support, or marketing execution. The goal is not to hire a mini-you who can do everything you do; it's to offload specific tasks that are taking your time away from high-value activities that only you can perform as the owner and primary strategist.

Start with contractors before committing to employees if possible because contractors provide flexibility without the legal and financial overhead of employment including payroll taxes, benefits, workers compensation insurance, and legal obligations around termination. You can scale contractor hours up and down with business volume, test working relationships before committing to permanent arrangements, and avoid the very significant costs of mis-hiring by simply ending contractor relationships that aren't working rather than going through termination processes. The downside is that contractors typically cost more per hour than employees and have less commitment to your business, potentially leaving for other opportunities without notice or refusing peak-volume work if they're busy with other clients.

Automation tools and technology multiply your effectiveness by handling repetitive tasks without human intervention, allowing a small team to accomplish what would traditionally require many more people. Email marketing automation sends targeted messages to customer segments based on their behaviors without manual intervention for each send, customer relationship management systems track all interactions and pipeline progress automatically rather than requiring manual note-taking and spreadsheet updates, accounting software categorizes transactions and generates financial reports with minimal manual bookkeeping, and scheduling tools eliminate the back-and-forth of finding meeting times. The initial setup investment in these tools pays for itself many times over through time savings and reduced errors compared to manual processes.

Build automation into your business from the beginning rather than waiting until operational chaos forces you to acknowledge you need better systems, because retrofitting automation into chaotic manual processes is far harder than building automated workflows from the start. Every time you find yourself doing the same task repeatedly, ask whether a tool or system could handle it automatically or at least make it dramatically more efficient. The hours you spend researching and implementing automation compound into massive time savings over months and years, essentially buying you additional hours in every day to focus on growth rather than operations.

Exit strategies and building sellable businesses might seem premature to think about when you're just starting, but understanding what makes a business valuable to potential buyers shapes decisions from day one that determine whether you're building an asset or just a job. Businesses that are attractive to buyers have several key characteristics: documented systems and processes that allow operations without the founder, diversified customer base without over-reliance on any single client, recurring revenue or predictable sales cycles rather than sporadic project work, strong market position or intellectual property that creates competitive advantages, and financial records that clearly demonstrate profitability and cash flow.

Even if you never intend to sell your business, building it as if you might sell eventually forces good practices that make it more profitable and less dependent on you personally, improving your quality of life and financial results regardless of your ultimate exit plan. A business built to be sellable can also be transitioned to family members, converted to a passive income stream managed by others, or simply run more profitably because it's not dependent on the founder's heroic daily efforts. The discipline of building systems, documenting processes, and creating genuine business value rather than just buying yourself a job creates better outcomes in every scenario, making it worth prioritizing even if selling is the furthest thing from your mind.

Actionable Takeaways

Entrepreneurship remains abstract and theoretical until you take concrete actions that transform ideas into actual businesses generating real revenue and solving genuine customer problems. The vast majority of aspiring entrepreneurs never start because they're waiting for perfect conditions or the ideal opportunity, not realizing that entrepreneurship is learned by doing and that their first venture will likely fail or at least require significant pivoting before it succeeds. Start now with whatever resources and knowledge you currently have, knowing that the learning from actually trying is infinitely more valuable than additional months of planning and preparation.

Business Idea Validation Checklist:
Before investing significant time or money in any business idea, work through this systematic validation process that tests your assumptions against market reality. First, identify the specific problem your business solves and articulate it clearly in one or two sentences that a potential customer would recognize as describing their frustration. Second, identify your target customer with demographic and psycho graphic specificity, describing exactly who experiences this problem and would pay to solve it. Third, research existing solutions and identify their specific weaknesses or gaps that your approach addresses better.

Fourth, conduct ten to fifteen customer interviews with people who fit your target profile, asking about their experiences with the problem and current solutions without pitching your idea, listening for validation that the problem is real and painful enough to warrant spending money. Fifth, determine whether people are already spending money trying to solve this problem, either through competing products or through inefficient workarounds that cost time and resources. Sixth, create a simple landing page describing your solution and drive one hundred targeted visitors to it, measuring what percentage provides their email for early access. If you can't get validation in each of these steps, your idea likely needs refinement or abandonment before you invest further.

Lean Startup Canvas:

Create a one-page business plan using the lean startup canvas framework that forces you to articulate your business model and key assumptions clearly without the bloat of traditional business plans. The canvas includes nine boxes covering problem, solution, key metrics, unique value proposition, unfair advantage, channels, customer segments, cost structure, and revenue streams. Fill out each section with your current best guesses, recognizing that these are hypotheses to be tested rather than certainties. This canvas becomes your road map for systematic validation, identifying which assumptions are most critical and risky so you can test them first before building too much on potentially false foundations.

Update your lean startup canvas every month based on what you learn from customer interactions and early traction, treating it as a living document that evolves as you gain knowledge rather than a static plan to be followed regardless of evidence. The canvas should change significantly in the first six months as you discover that some assumptions were wrong and others require refinement, with iterations becoming smaller as you find product-market fit and your understanding solidifies. This iterative approach prevents the common failure mode of rigid adherence to an initial plan that doesn't match market reality.

First Ninety Days Business Plan:

Create a detailed action plan for your first three months in business that focuses on validation and first revenue rather than perfect execution or premature scaling. Week one through four focus on setup and preparation: entity formation if needed, basic brand identity, simple website or landing page, initial marketing materials, and reaching out to your network announcing your new venture. Week five through eight focus on first customers: outreach to potential clients, service delivery or product creation for early adopters, gathering feedback and testimonials, and refining your offering based on real market response.

Week nine through twelve focus on systematic growth: implementing lessons from early customers, creating repeatable processes for acquisition and delivery, setting up basic automation and systems, and building pipeline for continued revenue in months two and three. Your goal at ninety days should be at least five to ten paying customers and monthly revenue of at least one to three thousand dollars depending on your business model, proving that people will actually pay for what you offer and that you can deliver profitably even if not efficiently yet. These modest milestones matter enormously because they represent validation that you have a real business rather than just an interesting idea.

Business Model Comparison Chart:

Systematically evaluate different business models you could pursue, comparing them across the dimensions that matter most for your situation and goals. Create a comparison chart with different business models across the top like consulting, software product, information products, e-commerce, agency services, and key evaluation criteria down the left side including startup capital required, time to first revenue, income potential at one year and five years, scalability, passive income potential, required ongoing time commitment, and alignment with your skills and interests. Rate each model on each dimension using a simple one-to-five scale, then calculate total scores to identify which models best fit your specific constraints and objectives.

This structured comparison prevents the common mistake of pursuing business models that sound exciting or profitable in the abstract but don't actually fit your resources, timeline, or capabilities. A software business might score high on scalability and passive income potential but low on time to first revenue and required technical skills if you're not a developer. A consulting business might score high on time to first revenue and leveraging existing skills but low on scalability and passive income potential. Neither model is inherently better; the right choice depends entirely on your specific situation, making objective comparison essential for making wise decisions rather than chasing shiny objects.

Building a successful business represents one of the most reliable paths to significant wealth for people willing to accept its risks and commit to the work required to succeed where most fail. The businesses that create wealth aren't usually the sexy startups featured in tech news but rather ordinary businesses solving real problems for paying customers, systematically built by entrepreneurs who focused on sustainable profitability rather than growth at any cost. Your entrepreneurial journey begins with a single step, one customer, one product, or one service that proves you can create value others will pay for. Everything else builds from that foundation of demonstrated value creation.

7

The Automatic Wealth System - Pay Yourself First

Section 1: Why Budgets Fail (And What Works Instead)

Traditional budgeting has failed millions of people who tried earnestly to track every expense, stay within category limits, and somehow maintain willpower across hundreds of daily spending decisions for months or years without breaking. The fundamental flaw in traditional budgeting is that it relies on constant conscious decision-making and sustained willpower to resist temptation repeatedly, fighting against human psychology and behavioral economics that make such sustained discipline nearly impossible for most people. Even highly motivated individuals with genuine commitment to financial goals find themselves breaking budgets regularly, then feeling guilty and defeated in ways that often lead to giving up entirely rather than finding better systems.

The psychology of restriction explains why budgets that feel like deprivation diets inevitably fail just like ninety-five percent of weight loss diets fail despite people's sincere desire to lose weight and willingness to try hard. When you tell yourself you cannot spend money on categories you enjoy, you create psychological reactance, the human tendency to want something more intensely when it's forbidden or restricted. This reactance builds over days and weeks of deprivation until it overwhelms your willpower in moments of weakness, leading to spending binges that undo weeks of careful restraint. The guilt and shame from these failures then make you less likely to return to budgeting, creating a destructive cycle of restriction, failure, guilt, and giving up.

Budget fatigue sets in when you're constantly monitoring spending across multiple categories, questioning every purchase decision, and feeling stressed about whether you're staying within limits rather than enjoying your life. The cognitive load of tracking spending in real-time and making constant calculations about whether you can afford things within your budget drains mental energy that could be better spent on work, relationships, or pursuing meaningful goals. This exhaustion eventually leads most people to stop tracking, stop caring, or convince themselves that budgeting doesn't work for them rather than recognizing that the budgeting method itself was flawed.

Automation versus willpower represents the fundamental principle that separates systems that work from systems that fail, acknowledging that humans are weak at sustained self-control but excellent at setting up systems that remove the need for constant decision-making. Willpower is a finite resource that depletes throughout the day and weakens when you're stressed, tired, hungry, or emotional, which is why relying on willpower for financial success means your financial outcomes depend on your momentary emotional and physical state rather than your actual goals and values. Automation removes willpower from the equation by making the right financial behaviors happen automatically without requiring any conscious decision or effort.

The power of automation becomes obvious when you consider that most people successfully save for retirement through employer-sponsored plans that automatically deduct contributions from paychecks before the money ever reaches checking accounts where it could be spent. These same people might completely fail to save money if they had to manually transfer funds from checking to retirement accounts each month, not because they don't value retirement but because the friction of manual action combined with the temptation to skip "just this month" creates failure points that automated systems eliminate. What works for retirement saving works equally well for all financial goals when you structure your money management around automation rather than willpower.

Reverse budgeting explained means flipping traditional budgeting on its head by automatically saving and investing first, then spending whatever remains guilt-free rather than trying to spend carefully all month and save whatever left over. Traditional budgeting assumes you'll control spending to create surplus for saving; reverse budgeting assumes you'll spend whatever available and therefore removes savings from the available pool before you have the chance to spend it. This simple reversal transforms saving from something requiring constant willpower into something that happens automatically regardless of your discipline or decision-making.

The reverse budgeting framework works because it acknowledges reality about human behavior rather than demanding we change our nature to fit an idealized system. Most people will spend approximately what's in their checking account regardless of intentions to save, either through conscious purchases or unconscious lifestyle inflation that somehow always absorbs available income. By removing savings before it enters the spending pool, reverse budgeting aligns the system with this tendency rather than fighting against it, ensuring savings happen first while removing the guilt from spending since you know your important financial obligations are already handled automatically.

The spending guilt-free approach that reverse budgeting enables might seem reckless to traditional personal finance advice, but it's actually psychologically healthier and more sustainable than constant restriction and monitoring.

When you know that your savings, investments, and important financial obligations are automatically handled before you see the money, you can spend what remains on things you enjoy without second-guessing every purchase or feeling guilty about treating yourself. This guilt-free spending within your automated system is far more sustainable than trying to restrict yourself constantly, preventing the binge-restrict cycle that destroys most budgeting attempts and allowing you to maintain financial discipline indefinitely rather than just until willpower inevitably fails.

Section 2: The Pay Yourself First Framework

Pay yourself first represents perhaps the single most important principle in wealth building, transforming the relationship between earning and saving from "save what's left after spending" to "spend what's left after saving." This principle sounds simple but its impact is profound because it ensures that wealth building happens automatically and consistently regardless of circumstances, expenses, or temptations that would otherwise prevent savings. When you pay yourself first, you treat your future self as the most important creditor who gets paid before anyone else including your current self, creating an automatic forcing function that builds wealth over time through consistency rather than sporadic contributions when you feel motivated or happen to have money left over.

Setting up automatic transfers removes the decision fatigue and potential failure points of manual savings, transforming good intentions into automatic behaviors that happen whether you remember them or not. Schedule automatic transfers from your checking account to savings and investment accounts on payday before you have time to spend the money, ensuring that wealth-building contributions happen first rather than competing with spending for whatever money remains at month's end. Most employers allow you to split direct deposit across multiple accounts, meaning your paycheck can automatically flow to checking for bills and spending, savings accounts for emergency funds and goals, and investment accounts for long-term wealth building without you touching or seeing most of the money.

The beauty of split direct deposit is that money you never see in your checking account never feels available to spend, preventing the lifestyle inflation that absorbs raises and bonuses if all income flows through a single account where it's visible and accessible. When you get a raise, immediately increase your automatic savings and investment contributions to capture at least fifty percent of the increase, allowing your lifestyle to improve modestly while ensuring that income growth translates to wealth growth rather than just spending growth. This one habit of automatically saving at least half of every raise compounds into enormous wealth differences over a career compared to people who spend every increase and wonder why their financial situation never improves despite earning more.

Percentage-based savings makes wealth building scalable to your income level rather than requiring fixed dollar amounts that might be easy for high earners but impossible for people with modest incomes. The fifty-thirty-twenty rule suggests allocating fifty percent of after-tax income to needs, thirty percent to wants, and twenty percent to savings and debt payoff, providing a simple framework that works reasonably well for many people though it's certainly not the only way to structure your finances. The specific percentages matter less than the principle of making savings a percentage of income rather than a fixed amount, ensuring that savings scales up automatically as your income grows rather than remaining stuck at whatever arbitrary dollar amount you started with.

For aggressive wealth building, consider increasing your savings rate beyond twenty percent toward fifty percent or more if your income and circumstances allow, dramatically accelerating your path to financial independence. Every ten percentage points increase in savings rate reduces the time to financial independence by several years, meaning someone saving fifty percent of income can potentially achieve financial independence in fifteen to seventeen years compared to thirty to forty years for someone saving ten percent. This relationship between savings rate and time to independence is mathematical and unavoidable, making increased savings rate the single most powerful lever for accelerating wealth building beyond just earning more or getting better investment returns.

High-yield savings accounts maximize the returns on cash you're holding for emergency funds or short-term goals, earning you hundreds or thousands of dollars in additional interest annually compared to traditional bank accounts paying essentially zero interest. As of this writing, high-yield savings accounts from online banks pay four to five percent interest while traditional bank savings accounts pay perhaps point-zero-one percent, a difference that seems small until you calculate the actual dollar impact on meaningful savings balances. Ten thousand dollars in a high-yield savings account earning four percent generates four hundred dollars annually in interest; that same ten thousand in a traditional bank account earns one dollar per year, a difference of three hundred ninety-nine dollars that compounds over time.

The only downside to high-yield savings accounts is that they're typically offered by online-only banks rather than traditional banks with physical branches, which makes some people nervous about accessing their money or dealing with issues. This concern is largely unfounded because these online banks are FDIC insured just like traditional banks, and electronic transfers between accounts typically take one to three business days which is perfectly acceptable for emergency fund money that you're not accessing regularly. The hundreds or thousands of dollars in additional interest you earn over years far outweighs any minor inconvenience of dealing with an online bank, making it foolish to leave emergency funds in traditional savings accounts earning nothing when high-yield alternatives are readily available.

Separate accounts for different goals prevent the common problem of co-mingling savings for multiple purposes, then spending from the combined pool without clear understanding of which goal you're robbing to fund current spending. When your emergency fund, house down payment savings, vacation fund, and car replacement fund all sit in one savings account, the total balance looks substantial but you've mentally spent it multiple times across different goals. This makes it easy to rationalize spending from the account for purposes that aren't really aligned with any of those goals, slowly draining the balance through a thousand small decisions rather than one conscious choice to abandon a goal.

Maintain separate savings accounts for each major goal with clear labels and specific target balances, making it impossible to spend vacation savings on impulse purchases without consciously deciding to raid that specific pool. Most banks allow you to create multiple savings accounts or sub-accounts at no additional cost, and many provide features for naming accounts and tracking progress toward goals. This separation provides psychological benefits beyond just organizational clarity because you can watch each goal account grow toward its target, creating motivation and satisfaction that's impossible when all savings are pooled together in one undifferentiated lump.

Section 3: Building Your Financial Cushion

Your emergency fund represents the foundation of financial security, providing a buffer against the unexpected expenses and income disruptions that derail financial plans and force people into debt despite their best intentions. Life is inherently unpredictable and expensive surprises are guaranteed to happen regularly, whether that's car repairs, medical bills, home maintenance, job losses, or any of the countless other financial emergencies that seem to always arrive at the worst possible times. Without an emergency fund, these inevitable surprises become crises that destroy your financial progress and often trigger spirals of debt that take years to escape. With an adequate emergency fund, the same events are inconvenient but manageable, handled with cash reserves rather than credit cards.

How much you really need in emergency savings is debated endlessly among personal finance experts, with recommendations ranging from one month to twelve months of expenses depending on who you ask and your specific situation. The standard recommendation of three to six months represents a reasonable middle ground for most employed people with stable jobs and dual incomes, providing meaningful protection without tying up so much cash that it significantly impacts your investing timeline. If you have irregular income from self-employment, commission-based sales, or seasonal work, you need closer to six to twelve months because your income volatility makes longer unemployed periods more likely and more difficult to predict.

Three-month versus six-month versus twelve-month reserves each serve different situations and risk profiles, making it important to honestly assess your personal circumstances rather than blindly following generic advice. Three months works for government employees with excellent job security, people with multiple income sources, or individuals with very low fixed expenses who could dramatically cut spending in emergencies. Six months is better for most people with normal employment, providing buffer for extended job searches in competitive markets and overlapping emergencies that deplete funds before they can be replenished. Twelve months is appropriate for single-income households where job loss would eliminate all income, people with health conditions that might prevent working, or extremely risk-averse individuals who value security over investment returns.

The calculation of months of expenses should be based on truly necessary spending rather than your current full spending including discretionary categories, because in a real emergency you would cut non-essential spending immediately to extend your runway. Calculate your bare-bones survival budget including rent or mortgage, basic groceries, utilities, insurance, minimum debt payments, and other truly non-negotiable expenses, then multiply by your target months of coverage. A household with four thousand monthly in total spending but only twenty-five hundred in truly essential expenses needs seven thousand five hundred to fifteen thousand for three to six months of emergency coverage, not twelve thousand to twenty-four thousand based on total spending.

Where to keep emergency money balances accessibility with earning reasonable returns, acknowledging that emergency funds must be immediately available without market risk but should still earn something rather than sitting in checking accounts earning nothing. High-yield savings accounts represent the optimal location for most emergency funds, providing FDIC insurance, immediate electronic access, and current interest rates of four to five percent that at least keep pace with inflation if not beat it. Money market accounts offer similar benefits and sometimes slightly higher rates, though the differences are usually minimal enough that either option works fine.

Some people suggest keeping a portion of emergency funds in very stable short-term bond funds or CDs for slightly higher returns, but this introduces either market risk or liquidity constraints that defeat the primary purpose of emergency funds. The few additional percentage points of return you might gain by putting emergency funds into higher-risk or less-liquid investments is not worth the possibility of needing the money during a market downturn and having to sell at losses, or having it locked in CDs when emergencies strike. Emergency funds should be boring and safe, optimized for availability and stability rather than returns, because their job is providing security not building wealth.

Fast access versus higher returns represents a trade-off where you should prioritize access for emergency funds, accepting lower returns in exchange for knowing the money is available instantly when needed. Your wealth building happens through retirement accounts and taxable investment accounts where you can accept market volatility and lock-up periods in exchange for higher long-term returns; your emergency fund is insurance against life's unpredictability, and insurance is supposed to cost you something in exchange for protection. The peace of mind from knowing you can handle emergencies without going into debt or liquidating investments at bad times is worth accepting the opportunity cost of keeping several months of expenses in cash rather than invested.

Many people make the mistake of under-funding emergency reserves in their eagerness to start investing, rationalizing that they could always sell investments if emergencies arise. This logic fails because emergencies often coincide with market downturns, as job losses cluster during recessions when markets are falling and selling investments locks in losses at the worst possible time. Having adequate emergency funds in cash prevents the forced selling that destroys wealth and allows you to stay invested through market volatility, ironically making you wealthier long-term despite the opportunity cost of keeping some money in low-return cash.

Section 4: Sinking Funds for Predictable Expenses

Sinking funds represent one of the most powerful but underutilized tools for avoiding the feast-or-famine financial stress that plagues people who treat predictable annual expenses as if they're unexpected emergencies. The concept is beautifully simple: identify expenses that occur annually or irregularly but predictably, calculate the total annual cost, divide by twelve, and save that amount monthly in dedicated accounts so the money is waiting when the expense arrives. This transforms expenses like holiday shopping, annual insurance premiums, property taxes, car registration, or home maintenance from budget-destroying surprises into planned expenses you've already saved for and can pay without stress or credit card debt.

Annual expenses that surprise you repeatedly are only surprises because you failed to plan for them, not because they're genuinely unexpected or unusual. Christmas happens every single year on the same date, yet millions of people act shocked when December arrives and they need to buy gifts, going into credit card debt to fund holiday spending that they absolutely knew was coming. Car registration fees, insurance premiums, and professional license renewals happen on predictable schedules that are typically known months in advance, yet people treat these expenses as emergencies rather than inevitable costs they should have been saving for monthly.

The psychology behind this failure to plan for predictable expenses is partially about present bias, our tendency to prioritize immediate needs and desires over future obligations, and partially about the pain of creating multiple savings buckets that feel restrictive and complicated. When your car registration is eight months away, setting aside thirty dollars monthly toward it feels unnecessary and even wasteful when you could spend that money on things you want right now. But when the registration notice arrives and you owe two hundred forty dollars immediately, you either scramble to find the money, put it on a credit card, or face consequences like fines or inability to legally drive.

Holiday spending fund should be a non-negotiable sinking fund for anyone who celebrates gift-giving holidays, calculating your typical holiday spending and dividing by twelve to determine your monthly contribution. If you typically spend twelve hundred dollars on holidays including gifts, decorations, travel, and special meals, you need to save one hundred dollars monthly starting in January so the money is available when November and December arrive. This advance saving means you can enjoy the holidays without the financial stress and credit card hangovers that ruin January for millions of people who financed their holiday celebration at twenty percent interest and are now paying for it for months while the joy of the season is long gone.

The beauty of a holiday sinking fund is that it removes the anxiety and guilt from holiday spending because you're using money you've already saved specifically for this purpose rather than borrowing from your future or choosing between gifts and bills. You can be generous with people you care about, participate in traditions that matter to you, and enjoy the season knowing that you planned ahead and paid for everything with cash. This advance planning also often reduces total spending because you're not making stressed last-minute purchases or financing things you can't really afford, instead making thoughtful choices about how to allocate the funds you've saved.

Car maintenance and replacement represents another perfect application of sinking funds because car expenses are absolutely predictable in aggregate even though specific repairs might surprise you with timing or cost. Your car will need regular maintenance like oil changes, tire rotations, and brake work on predictable schedules, and it will eventually need replacement either through catastrophic failure or simple age-related wear. By saving a fixed amount monthly for car expenses, you build a reserve that covers routine maintenance as it occurs and accumulates toward eventual replacement, preventing both types of car expenses from becoming financial emergencies.

Calculate your car sinking fund contribution by adding your annual maintenance costs, prorating major expenses like tire replacement over their lifespan, and adding a monthly amount toward replacement based on how long you plan to keep the car and how much you'll need to buy the next one. If your annual maintenance runs about twelve hundred dollars, tires cost eight hundred every four years, and you plan to replace the car in six years needing a six thousand dollar down payment, your monthly car sinking fund should be approximately two hundred dollars, covering routine costs while building toward major expenses. This might feel like a lot monthly, but it's simply making explicit and systematic the car costs you're going to incur anyway instead of pretending they won't happen until they do.

Home repairs and appliances sinking fund protects homeowners from the financial chaos of major unexpected repairs or appliance replacements that can cost thousands of dollars and seem to always arrive at the worst possible times. Water heaters, HVAC systems, refrigerators, and other major appliances all have predictable lifespans and will eventually need replacement; roofs, siding, and other home systems will eventually require major repairs or replacement regardless of how well maintained. These expenses aren't really unexpected; they're just irregular enough that homeowners fool themselves into believing their particular appliances will somehow last forever or that they'll worry about replacement when the time comes.

A reasonable home maintenance sinking fund contribution is one to two percent of your home's value annually, or approximately one hundred to two hundred dollars monthly for a two hundred forty thousand dollar home. This might seem like a lot to set aside for expenses that might not occur this year or next, but over time this fund builds a cushion that turns major home repairs from financial disasters into manageable expenses you've already saved for. When your water heater dies or your HVAC system needs replacement, you write a check from your home maintenance fund rather than putting five thousand dollars on a credit card or depleting your emergency fund for an expense that wasn't really an emergency but rather an inevitable event you should have planned for.

Actionable Takeaways

The automated wealth system you've learned in this chapter transforms from theoretical knowledge into actual wealth only through implementation, through setting up the accounts, automating the transfers, and committing to the system even when immediate temptations suggest spending money you've earmarked for savings. Most people who read about automation and pay-yourself-first principles nod along in agreement but never actually set up the systems, remaining stuck in the willpower-based budgeting approaches that have failed them repeatedly. This week, not next month or when things slow down or after you pay off that one thing, you need to implement these systems so they start building wealth automatically regardless of your future motivation or discipline.

Automatic Savings Setup Guide:

Transform your theoretical understanding of automation into actual working systems within the next seven days by completing these specific setup tasks. First, calculate your target savings rate as a percentage of take-home pay, starting with at least twenty percent if possible or working toward that target if your current budget is too tight. Second, log into your employer's payroll system and set up direct deposit splitting to automatically send your savings percentage to a separate high-yield savings account before the money reaches your primary checking account. If your employer doesn't offer split deposit, set up automatic transfers from your checking account to savings on the same day your paycheck deposits, removing the money before you have time to spend it.

Third, open a high-yield savings account with an online bank if you don't already have one, researching current rates and choosing an account paying at least four percent or whatever the current competitive rate is at time of reading. Fourth, create separate savings accounts or sub-accounts for emergency fund, sinking funds for annual expenses, and any specific savings goals like down payments or vacations, naming each account clearly so you know what the money is for. Fifth, calculate monthly contributions to each sinking fund based on annual expenses divided by twelve, setting up automatic monthly transfers on payday so these savings happen systematically rather than whenever you remember.

Emergency Fund Calculator:

Determine your specific emergency fund target based on your actual circumstances rather than generic rules, then create a plan for reaching that target within a reasonable time frame. First, calculate your bare-bones monthly expenses including only truly non-negotiable costs like housing, utilities, food, insurance, minimum debt payments, and other things you absolutely cannot eliminate even in severe financial stress. Second, multiply that monthly amount by three, six, or twelve months depending on your employment stability, income sources, and personal risk tolerance, giving you a specific dollar target for your full emergency fund.

Third, if you're starting from zero or have minimal savings, commit to building a starter emergency fund of one thousand dollars before focusing on other financial goals beyond minimum debt payments, giving you basic protection against small emergencies. Fourth, once you have your starter fund, calculate how much you need to save monthly to reach your full emergency fund target within twelve to twenty-four months, balancing aggressive emergency fund building with debt payoff and other priorities. Fifth, automate these monthly emergency fund contributions and resist the temptation to raid the fund for non-emergencies, remembering that its purpose is providing security and preventing debt when real emergencies strike.

Sinking Fund Tracker:

Create a comprehensive system for identifying all your irregular expenses and funding them systematically rather than being surprised when they arrive. First, review your past twelve months of spending and identify every expense over one hundred dollars that occurs annually or irregularly, including things like insurance premiums, car registration, property taxes, professional memberships, subscription renewals, holiday spending, and any other costs that arrive less frequently than monthly. Second, estimate the annual cost of each expense, being conservative and rounding up rather than optimistically underestimating.

Third, create a simple spreadsheet listing each sinking fund category, the annual amount needed, the monthly contribution required, and the current balance in that fund, giving you a dashboard of all your irregular expense planning in one place. Fourth, set up automatic monthly transfers for each sinking fund category, either using separate accounts if your bank allows multiple savings accounts or using a single account with tracking in your spreadsheet. Fifth, review and update your sinking fund tracker quarterly, adjusting contribution amounts if your spending patterns change or if accumulated balances in one fund could be better deployed toward other needs.

Account Structure Blueprint:

Design and implement an account structure that makes wealth building automatic and spending decisions simple rather than requiring constant monitoring and discipline. First, maintain at least three separate accounts: primary checking for bills and fixed expenses, secondary checking or prepaid card for discretionary spending, and high-yield savings for emergency funds and sinking funds. Second, set up your paycheck to automatically split across these accounts based on your budget, with fixed percentages going to bills, discretionary spending, and savings so the division happens automatically without requiring monthly transfers or decision-making.

Third, configure automatic payments for all fixed bills from your primary checking account, ensuring that rent or mortgage, utilities, insurance, minimum debt payments, and other non-negotiable expenses pay themselves without manual intervention each month. Fourth, load your discretionary spending account with a fixed weekly or monthly amount based on your budget, using that account for all restaurants, entertainment, shopping, and other variable expenses, knowing that when the balance hits zero you stop discretionary spending until the next reload. Fifth, never touch your savings accounts for regular spending, treating that money as completely unavailable unless you're facing a genuine emergency or the specific purpose you saved for has arrived.

The automatic wealth system works not because it requires superhuman discipline or perfect execution but because it removes the need for discipline entirely, making the right financial behaviors happen automatically while allowing you to live your life without constant financial stress or monitoring. You will build wealth faster through mediocre automation than through perfect manual budgeting because consistency matters far more than optimization, and automated systems achieve consistency that willpower-based approaches never can. Set up these systems this week and watch your wealth grow automatically month after month, year after year, regardless of how motivated or disciplined you feel in any particular moment.

8

High-Impact Frugality - Living Rich While Spending Less

Section 1: Strategic vs. Stupid Frugality

The frugality movement has created two distinct camps that represent fundamentally different philosophies about money and life, with one camp building genuine wealth through strategic spending cuts while the other wastes enormous time and energy on penny-pinching that makes almost no mathematical difference to their financial outcomes. Understanding the difference between strategic frugality that accelerates wealth building and stupid frugality that makes you miserable without meaningfully improving your finances is crucial for deploying your limited time and willpower where they'll actually create results rather than just making you feel virtuous about saving nickels while hemorrhaging dollars elsewhere.

The eighty-twenty principle of money-saving states that roughly twenty percent of your spending categories account for eighty percent of your total spending, making those categories the only ones where spending cuts create meaningful financial impact. For most people, housing, transportation, and food represent well over half of total spending, meaning that a ten percent reduction in these categories saves far more money than completely eliminating smaller expenses like coffee, subscriptions, or entertainment. Yet most frugality advice focuses obsessively on the small stuff, encouraging people to make their own laundry detergent or skip coffee shop visits while ignoring the thousands of dollars they could save monthly by getting a roommate or driving a cheaper car.

Big wins versus penny-pinching means focusing your optimization efforts on the largest expense categories where even modest percentage reductions create substantial dollar savings, rather than exhausting yourself trying to minimize every small expense and making your life miserable in the process. Cutting your housing cost from two thousand to fifteen hundred dollars monthly saves six thousand dollars annually, the equivalent of eliminating one hundred dollars in small monthly expenses, but the housing reduction requires just one decision and effort while the small expenses require constant vigilance and hundreds of individual choices to skip things you might enjoy. The mathematical superiority of focusing on big expenses is undeniable, yet cultural messaging and personal finance media continue emphasizing small daily expenses because they're easier to write about than the harder truths about housing and transportation costs.

This focus on big wins doesn't mean small expenses never matter or that you should spend recklessly on daily purchases, but it does mean that your primary optimization focus should be housing, transportation, and food until you've minimized those categories, and only then should you worry about optimizing smaller spending areas. Someone paying three thousand monthly for housing, six hundred for car payments and insurance, and eight hundred for food while agonizing over whether to spend five dollars on coffee is optimizing in completely the wrong order. Get housing to fifteen hundred, transportation to three hundred, and food to five hundred through strategic moves, and you've freed up twenty-five hundred dollars monthly, or thirty thousand dollars annually, that can be redirected toward wealth building regardless of how much you spend on coffee.

Quality of life preservation separates strategic frugality from the miserable deprivation that most people imagine when they hear about living below your means, acknowledging that the goal is building wealth to create a better life, not destroying your current life in service of some distant financial goal you might never reach. Strategic frugality maintains or even improves quality of life by cutting expenses on things that don't actually bring you joy or value while continuing to spend freely on things that genuinely matter to your happiness and well being. This requires honest self-assessment about what spending actually makes your life better versus what spending is just habit, social expectation, or attempts to fill emotional voids that money can't actually fill.

The key insight is that much of our spending provides minimal actual satisfaction relative to its cost, meaning we can cut that spending without sacrificing anything we truly value or enjoy. Most people have gym memberships they rarely use, subscriptions they forgot about, possessions they never touch, convenience purchases that barely save time, and social spending they'd gladly skip if given permission. Eliminating this zero-value spending hurts nothing except perhaps your ego or social image, freeing up hundreds or thousands of dollars monthly without any actual reduction in life satisfaction. Meanwhile, spending on things you genuinely value and enjoy should generally continue unless those things are financially catastrophic, because wealth building should serve your life rather than consuming it.

Value-based spending means aligning your spending with your actual values and priorities rather than defaulting to whatever society, advertising, or your peer group suggests you should spend money on. If you genuinely value experiences over possessions, spending thousands on travel while living cheaply at home and driving an old car makes perfect sense; if you value possessions over experiences, the opposite allocation might be right for you. If you love cooking and food is a genuine passion, spending more on groceries and kitchen equipment while cutting other areas is completely reasonable; if you view food purely as fuel, spending hundreds on fancy meals and premium ingredients is waste that should be redirected elsewhere.

Most people never do this values alignment work and instead spend based on habit, convenience, social pressure, and emotional impulses, which is why they can simultaneously feel broke and spend enormous amounts on things that don't actually matter to them. Take time to identify your true values and the experiences or possessions that genuinely bring you satisfaction, then ruthlessly cut spending in areas that don't serve those values while maintaining or even increasing spending on what matters most. This approach creates a lifestyle that feels abundant and satisfying despite lower total spending because you're concentrating resources where they actually impact your well being rather than diffusing them across countless things that make minimal difference.

Section 2: The Big Three - Housing, Transportation, Food

Housing represents the single largest expense for most households and therefore the greatest opportunity for meaningful spending reduction, yet it's also the expense most people resist examining critically because moving or changing living situations feels overwhelming compared to just complaining about high rent or mortgage payments. The reality is that housing costs are largely discretionary despite feeling fixed because you have enormous control over where you live, how much space you occupy, whether you live alone or with others, and what neighborhood or city you call home. These choices collectively determine whether you spend one thousand or four thousand monthly on housing, a difference of thirty-six thousand dollars annually that compounds into millions over a career.

Housing hacks that save five hundred to two thousand monthly start with the simplest but often most psychologically difficult option of getting roommates or housemates to split costs, transforming an expensive solo living situation into an affordable shared one. A two-bedroom apartment that costs two thousand monthly might cost twelve hundred to split between two people, saving each person eight hundred monthly or ninety-six hundred annually compared to each renting one-bedroom units. This single decision to accept roommates can save more money annually than most side hustles generate and requires zero ongoing effort beyond the initial roommate search, yet millions of people reject this option out of hand because they've decided they're too old or too established to share housing despite the enormous financial penalty they're paying for privacy.

The roommate objection usually centers on privacy, lifestyle compatibility, and feeling like sharing housing is regressing to college rather than demonstrating adult success, but these psychological barriers cost tens or hundreds of thousands of dollars over time for benefits that might not actually improve well being as much as financial security would. Many people who reluctantly accept roommates for financial reasons discover they actually enjoy the company and social connection more than they valued the privacy they thought was essential, while others maintain perfectly functional roommate situations by choosing compatible people and establishing clear boundaries about shared versus private spaces and times. Even if you genuinely hate having roommates, the question isn't whether you'd prefer living alone; it's whether you'd prefer living alone or being financially independent ten years earlier, because that's often the actual trade-off you're making.

Moving to a cheaper neighborhood, suburb, or city represents another high-impact housing strategy that can save hundreds or thousands monthly, though it requires accepting trade-offs in commute time, neighborhood amenities, or social prestige. A trendy downtown apartment might cost three thousand monthly while a perfectly adequate apartment twenty minutes away costs eighteen hundred, saving fourteen thousand annually for the inconvenience of a longer commute or less walk able neighborhood. This financial difference is so large that it can fund a comfortable retirement decades earlier or eliminate debt in years rather than decades, yet many people refuse to even consider cheaper areas because they've mentally committed to living in particular neighborhoods that their incomes don't actually support without financial stress.

The decision about where to live should be explicitly financial rather than just emotional or social, calculating the total cost including rent or mortgage, utilities, parking, and commute expenses, then comparing that total to your income and wealth-building goals to determine whether your housing choice is aligned with your stated financial priorities. If you claim wealth building is important but you're spending forty percent of income on housing to live in a neighborhood that provides minimal concrete benefit beyond status or habit, your actions aren't aligned with your goals and one of them needs to change. Either accept that housing preference is more important than wealth building and stop feeling anxious about finances, or prioritize wealth building and move somewhere cheaper regardless of how that feels emotionally or what people might think.

Downsizing from larger than necessary space to smaller adequate space can save hundreds monthly on rent or mortgage while also reducing utilities, maintenance, and the tendency to accumulate possessions to fill empty rooms. Many people live in three-bedroom houses or apartments when they functionally use only one or two bedrooms, paying a premium for space that serves no purpose beyond housing junk or providing guest rooms that see visitors once or twice yearly. A single person paying eighteen hundred for a two-bedroom apartment when one-bedrooms in the same building rent for thirteen hundred is wasting six thousand dollars annually on unused space, money that could eliminate debt or build substantial investment portfolios over time.

The psychological resistance to downsizing often centers on loss aversion and identity, feeling like moving to a smaller space represents failure or regression rather than a strategic financial decision that creates options and reduces stress. This framing is completely backward because what actually represents failure is being trapped in expensive housing you can't comfortably afford, stressed about money constantly, unable to build wealth or pursue opportunities because your housing costs consume too much income. Living in a smaller space you can easily afford while building wealth and options represents success and wisdom, not failure, regardless of what size-obsessed culture might suggest about the importance of square footage to life satisfaction.

Transportation costs represent the second-largest expense category for most households and one of the biggest gaps between what people think they need and what they actually need to function well. The average new car payment in America exceeds six hundred dollars monthly before insurance and fuel, meaning transportation costs for many households exceed one thousand monthly or twelve thousand annually, yet most of these people could meet their actual transportation needs with vehicles costing a fraction of that amount. The difference between driving a forty thousand dollar car and a ten thousand dollar reliable used car is approximately five hundred dollars monthly in payments alone, or six thousand annually, plus hundreds more in insurance and registration costs for the more expensive vehicle.

Car ownership optimization starts with the fundamental question of whether you actually need to own a car at all or whether public transportation, bikes, walking, or ride-sharing could meet your transportation needs at a fraction of car ownership costs. Monthly car ownership including payment, insurance, fuel, maintenance, parking, and registration typically exceeds six hundred dollars and often approaches one thousand, while comparable transportation through other means usually costs two hundred to four hundred monthly depending on your location and usage patterns. The six hundred dollar monthly savings from not owning a car amounts to seventy-two hundred dollars annually or over one hundred forty thousand dollars over twenty years before accounting for investment returns, a difference that could fund several years of retirement or a house down payment.

For people who genuinely need cars for work or family logistics, the optimization question becomes how little you can spend on reliable transportation rather than how much car you can afford in monthly payments. A seven-year-old Honda Civic with one hundred thousand miles costs perhaps eight thousand dollars and will likely run for another one hundred thousand miles with basic maintenance, providing reliable transportation for a fraction of what people spend on new car payments. The psychological desire for new cars, fancy features, or vehicles that signal status rather than just transport you reliably costs most people hundreds of thousands of dollars over their lives, money that would generate more actual well being if invested toward financial independence than it generates through nicer cars they barely notice after the first few weeks of ownership.

The one-car family strategy saves enormous money for households that defaulted to two-car ownership without seriously considering whether coordinating schedules and occasionally using ride-sharing for conflicts might be worth saving six thousand to twelve thousand annually in second-car expenses. Many two-car households could function as one-car families with modest coordination effort, perhaps one spouse biking or taking transit to work or both adults working from home enough that transportation coordination isn't difficult. The mental shift required is viewing the second car as costing you its full ownership expense annually rather than just whatever incremental gas and maintenance it requires, making the cost-benefit analysis clear enough to motivate the coordination effort if you're serious about wealth building.

Food spending represents the third major expense category and one where most people waste enormous amounts without realizing it through restaurant meals, convenience purchases, food waste, and failure to plan purchases strategically. The average American household spends over six hundred dollars monthly on food including groceries and restaurants, with many higher-income households spending one thousand or more, yet adequate nutrition costs perhaps three hundred to four hundred monthly when approached strategically through meal planning, bulk purchases, and cooking at home. The gap between what people spend and what food actually needs to cost represents hundreds of dollars monthly or thousands annually that could accelerate debt payoff or wealth building substantially.

Restaurant spending optimization doesn't require completely eliminating dining out if you genuinely enjoy it, but it does require conscious decision-making about which restaurant experiences actually provide value worth their cost versus which are just habit or convenience. Many people spend two hundred to four hundred monthly on restaurant meals without particularly enjoying most of them, eating out because they're tired, didn't plan meals, or defaulted to social expectations rather than because the food or experience was meaningfully better than home cooking. Strategic restaurant spending means limiting dining out to occasions that are genuinely special or social rather than routine fuel consumption, potentially cutting restaurant spending by seventy-five percent while maintaining or improving quality of life because the remaining restaurant experiences are chosen intentionally rather than occurring by default.

Grocery shopping strategic approaches center on planning meals weekly before shopping, creating detailed lists based on those meal plans, buying mostly whole ingredients rather than prepared foods, purchasing proteins and bulk items when on sale, and rigidly avoiding impulse purchases beyond the list. These tactics aren't secret knowledge and most people know they should do these things, but the gap between knowledge and execution creates the difference between spending three hundred monthly on groceries versus six hundred, with the discipline to actually plan and stick to lists being more valuable than any specific shopping hacks or couponing strategies. Someone who meal plans, lists, and avoids impulse purchases at a regular grocery store will spend far less than someone who shops randomly at discount stores, because the planning matters more than the store.

Meal planning and cooking at home requires time investment that many busy people resist, viewing cooking as drudgery competing with more enjoyable uses of their limited free time. This calculation often fails to account for the full cost of convenience, both financial and health-related, because restaurant meals cost three to five times what home cooking costs while typically being less healthy and less aligned with specific dietary preferences. The thirty to sixty minutes invested in cooking dinner saves perhaps twenty dollars versus dining out while providing healthier food and building a skill that compounds in value over time, representing an extremely high return on time investment that most people would recognize if they calculated it honestly.

Batch cooking and meal prep multiplies the efficiency of home cooking time by preparing multiple meals in one cooking session, transforming the time investment from daily to weekly while ensuring that healthy food is available when you're tired or busy rather than defaulting to expensive takeout. Spending three hours on Sunday preparing proteins, cutting vegetables, and cooking grains that you assemble into meals throughout the week requires less total time than cooking from scratch daily while making it far more likely you'll actually eat at home rather than ordering food out of exhaustion or lack of preparation. This strategy is particularly powerful for people who claim they don't have time to cook, because the time excuse usually means they don't have time or energy to cook from scratch nightly, but they do have time weekly to batch prepare components.

Section 3: Lifestyle Design on Any Budget

Geographic arbitrage for cost of living represents one of the most powerful wealth-building strategies available to people who can work remotely or find employment in multiple locations, allowing you to earn coastal salaries while living in low-cost areas where that income provides dramatically more purchasing power and wealth-building capacity. The difference in cost of living between expensive cities like San Francisco or New York and affordable cities in the Midwest or South can easily be fifty percent or more on major expenses like housing, making a hundred thousand dollar salary in San Francisco equivalent to perhaps sixty thousand in purchasing power after accounting for housing and living costs, while that same hundred thousand in a low-cost city might provide purchasing power equivalent to one hundred thirty thousand or more.

The mathematics of geographic arbitrage compound powerfully over time because the savings from lower living costs get invested and grow, creating wealth accumulation that's simply impossible for people earning the same income in expensive cities where nearly all income goes to living expenses. Someone earning ninety thousand in a low-cost area where housing costs eight hundred monthly and saving forty percent of income builds wealth far faster than someone earning one hundred twenty thousand in an expensive city where housing costs three thousand monthly and savings might be ten percent of income despite the higher absolute salary. The lower-paid worker in the cheaper location is saving three thousand monthly compared to one thousand monthly for the higher-paid worker in the expensive city, a difference that compounds into millions over a career.

The objection to geographic arbitrage usually centers on career opportunities, cultural amenities, or social networks that people believe exist only in expensive cities and justify the enormous financial penalty of living there. This logic made perfect sense before remote work became widely accepted, when certain industries like tech, finance, or entertainment essentially required living in specific expensive cities to access opportunities. But the explosion of remote work since the pandemic has fundamentally changed this calculation, making it increasingly possible to earn high salaries while living anywhere with reliable internet, eliminating the forced choice between career and cost of living.

For people in industries or roles where remote work isn't an option, the geographic arbitrage question becomes whether the career premium for expensive cities actually exceeds the cost-of-living penalty enough to make financial sense. If you can earn one hundred fifty thousand in San Francisco versus one hundred thousand in Austin, but your cost of living is thirty thousand higher in San Francisco, you're actually worse off financially despite the higher absolute salary. Only if the salary premium exceeds the cost-of-living difference plus some additional amount to compensate for the lifestyle and space sacrifices does the expensive city make financial sense, and for many people the math doesn't actually work out favorably when calculated honestly.

House hacking represents one of the most powerful wealth-building strategies available to homeowners willing to sacrifice some privacy and convenience in exchange for dramatically reduced or eliminated housing costs. The basic concept involves purchasing a multifamily property like a duplex, triplex, or fourplex, living in one unit while renting the others to cover most or all of your mortgage and expense, essentially living for free or even cash-flowing positively while building equity through tenants paying down your mortgage. This strategy can turn housing from your largest expense into either zero cost or actually an income source while you simultaneously build equity and force appreciation through property improvements.

The execution of house hacking requires purchasing properties in the right price range and location where rents will cover most of your mortgage, screening and managing tenants competently, maintaining the property properly, and accepting the reduction in privacy and increase in responsibility that comes from being a landlord while living in the same building. For people willing to accept these trade-offs, typically young professionals or families willing to sacrifice privacy temporarily for long-term wealth, house hacking can accelerate wealth building by five to ten years compared to traditional home ownership where you pay full housing costs from income, and by even more compared to renting without building any equity.

Accessory dwelling units allow single-family homeowners to house hack by adding legal secondary dwelling units to their properties, either through converting garages, building backyard cottages, or finishing basements into separate rental units. These ADUs can generate enough rent to cover substantial portions of mortgage payments while providing more privacy than traditional multifamily house hacking since the tenant isn't sharing walls or common areas as closely. The upfront investment to build or convert an ADU typically ranges from forty thousand to one hundred fifty thousand depending on location and project scope, but the ongoing rental income of one thousand to two thousand monthly often provides returns that far exceed traditional investments while simultaneously building home equity.

Travel hacking and credit card rewards provide savvy consumers with the ability to fund travel and experiences worth thousands of dollars annually using credit card sign up bonuses and rewards points rather than cash, though this strategy requires discipline around credit card usage to avoid interest charges that would completely negate any rewards value. The key to successful travel hacking is signing up for credit cards with large sign up bonuses, hitting the minimum spending requirements through normal expenses you'd have anyway, never carrying balances that would accrue interest, and maximizing rewards through strategic category spending where cards offer bonus points. Done correctly, this allows people to fund significant travel completely through points and miles that would have cost thousands in cash.

The warnings about travel hacking center on the risks of overspending to hit signup bonuses, accumulating credit card debt while chasing rewards, damaging credit through excessive applications, or missing payments and negating rewards value through interest charges and fees. These risks are real and have destroyed the finances of people who got caught up in rewards optimization without maintaining discipline around spending and payments, which is why travel hacking is suitable only for people who already manage credit cards responsibly and won't be tempted into spending they can't afford by the lure of rewards. For these disciplined users, rewards can fund experiences worth three thousand to ten thousand annually, effectively increasing their lifestyle budget without increasing spending.

Free and low-cost entertainment challenges the assumption that enjoying life requires spending substantial money on restaurants, events, tickets, and entertainment, when many of the most satisfying experiences cost nothing or very little when approached creatively. Free entertainment abounds in most communities through library programs, community events, parks and nature areas, free museum days, local festivals, volunteer opportunities that provide social connection while serving others, exercise through walking or running outdoors, and social gatherings hosted at homes rather than restaurants and bars. The shift from paid to free entertainment requires initial effort to identify opportunities and sometimes advance planning since free events won't spontaneously occur when you're bored, but the financial savings of hundreds monthly paired with often higher-quality experiences than defaulting to whatever commercial entertainment is convenient makes this shift extremely high-value.

Low-cost alternatives to expensive entertainment habits can provide similar satisfaction at fractions of the cost when you question whether you're paying for the actual experience or just the convenience and social expectations surrounding how people are supposed to spend leisure time. Home movie nights cost perhaps twenty dollars for snacks versus eighty dollars for theater tickets and concessions; hiking at local trails costs zero compared to fifty dollars for gym memberships or entry fees to attractions; potluck dinners with friends cost ten dollars per person versus fifty to one hundred for comparable restaurant meals; community sports leagues cost one hundred annually versus thousands for boutique fitness classes. None of these substitutions represent deprivation if you're getting similar social connection, entertainment, or fitness benefits at a fraction of the cost.

Section 4: Avoiding Lifestyle Inflation

Lifestyle inflation represents the single biggest reason most people never achieve financial independence despite earning good incomes, as they unconsciously increase spending to match income increases rather than maintaining their previous lifestyle while investing the difference. This pattern plays out predictably across income levels, with people earning forty thousand or two hundred thousand equally likely to feel they have no money left after expenses because they've allowed their lifestyle to consume every increase. The natural human tendency to adapt quickly to higher living standards while forgetting previous satisfaction at lower levels makes lifestyle inflation almost automatic unless you create systems and commitments to prevent it.

The raise trap works like this: you get a ten percent raise from fifty thousand to fifty-five thousand, increasing your annual income by five thousand dollars. This feels exciting initially because five thousand is real money that could make a meaningful difference to your financial situation if saved and invested. But within months of the raise, your lifestyle has somehow expanded to consume the increase through some combination of eating out more, upgrading subscriptions, buying nicer clothes, or moving to a slightly better apartment. By the end of the first year, you can't actually identify where that five thousand went, and you feel no wealthier despite earning significantly more than before the raise.

This unconscious lifestyle expansion happens because the raise feels like permission to spend more rather than an opportunity to build wealth faster, and because small daily increases in spending from the slightly increased income add up to consume the entire raise without any single purchase feeling significant enough to reconsider. The five thousand annually breaks down to about four hundred monthly or ninety-two weekly, amounts that disappear easily through slightly more expensive coffee, more frequent restaurant meals, premium grocery purchases rather than store brands, streaming subscriptions you didn't have before, or any of countless small upgrades that individually seem trivial but collectively consume every penny of increased earnings.

Breaking the raise trap requires deliberate commitments made before raises occur rather than trusting yourself to save increase income when it arrives and spending temptations are strongest. The most effective strategy is immediately increasing your automatic savings and investment contributions by at least fifty percent of any raise, capturing that wealth-building benefit before lifestyle creep can consume it. A five thousand dollar raise should trigger an automatic twenty-five hundred dollar increase in annual savings, allowing your lifestyle to improve by the remaining twenty-five hundred which feels good without preventing wealth building from accelerating. This automatic increase removes the decision from your stressed or tempted future self, making wealth building happen regardless of whether you feel like saving when the fatter paychecks start arriving.

Maintaining your enough threshold means identifying the income level and lifestyle that actually makes you satisfied, then consciously choosing to keep spending at approximately that level even as income rises rather than continuously chasing a moving target of enough that stays perpetually out of reach. The concept of enough is challenging for people raised in consumer culture that constantly messages that more is always better, that last year's luxuries are this year's necessities, and that your worth and success are measured by your visible consumption level. This messaging ensures most people never feel they have enough regardless of income because the target for enough keeps moving upward as income increases.

Research on happiness and income consistently shows that beyond about seventy-five thousand to one hundred thousand dollars annually, additional income produces minimal increases in day-to-day happiness though it continues improving life satisfaction and reducing financial stress. This suggests there's an enough threshold for most people where additional income beyond that level doesn't actually make daily life more enjoyable even though it provides security and options. Identifying your personal enough and committing to maintain lifestyle around that level while investing all income above it provides the psychological benefits of adequate income while capturing the wealth-building power of high savings rates that create genuine financial freedom.

Selective upgrades that matter allow for thoughtful lifestyle improvements in areas that genuinely enhance well being while maintaining discipline in areas where spending provides minimal benefit, creating a lifestyle that feels abundant where it counts without wasteful spending across all categories. This approach requires honest self-knowledge about what actually makes your life better versus what spending is just habit, social expectation, or mistaken beliefs about what will make you happy. For someone who loves cooking, upgrading kitchen equipment and ingredients while maintaining cheap housing and transportation might create more satisfaction than the reverse; for someone who doesn't care about food, expensive kitchens and groceries represent waste while upgraded living space or vehicles might provide genuine value.

The key is to consciously choose the few areas where upgraded spending genuinely improves your life and go ahead and spend there without guilt, while ruthlessly cutting everything else that doesn't provide comparable benefit. This creates a life with genuine luxuries you appreciate in the areas you care about while avoiding the diffuse mediocre spending across all categories that consumes high income without creating corresponding satisfaction. Someone might maintain budget housing and transportation while spending freely on hobbies and experiences they love, creating a rich life by their own values despite modest total spending because the spending is concentrated where it matters rather than spread evenly across categories.

Keeping up with yourself, not the Joneses, means competing against your own previous state and goals rather than comparing your visible consumption and lifestyle to peers whose financial situations you don't actually understand. Social comparison is hardwired into human psychology and naturally extends to financial life where we judge our own adequacy based on how our lifestyle compares to those around us, creating pressure to match peers' spending even when their financial situations are completely different from ours. This comparison almost always makes you feel inadequate because you're comparing your full financial reality including debts and stress to other people's curated public presentations that show only assets and consumption while hiding liabilities and anxiety.

The only competition that matters is whether you're doing better than your previous self, whether your net worth is growing, whether you're closer to financial independence than last year, and whether your financial stress is decreasing even if your absolute wealth isn't yet impressive. Comparing yourself to where you were a year ago rather than to peers whose situations you don't understand keeps you focused on your actual progress and goals rather than chasing a moving target of enough defined by others. This internal rather than external benchmark also helps resist lifestyle inflation because you can see clearly whether current spending is higher than necessary by comparing it to previous satisfaction at lower spending levels rather than constantly adjusting your baseline based on what peers appear to be spending.

Actionable Takeaways

Strategic frugality transforms from theoretical knowledge into actual wealth building through specific actions that reduce major expense categories while maintaining quality of life, not through vague intentions to spend less or generic advice to make coffee at home. The difference between people who successfully build wealth through controlled spending and those who remain stuck despite knowing they should spend less is concrete implementation of big-win strategies rather than diffuse attempts to be generally more frugal. This week you need to take action on at least one major expense category, making decisions and changes that will save hundreds or thousands annually rather than just thinking about what you should do differently.

High-Impact Savings Calculator:

Systematically identify exactly how much you could save by optimizing your three largest expense categories of housing, transportation, and food using realistic scenarios based on your current situation. First, calculate your current all-in housing cost including rent or mortgage, utilities, parking, and any other occupancy expenses, then calculate potential savings from realistic alternatives like getting a roommate, moving to a cheaper neighborhood, or downsizing to smaller adequate space. Second, calculate your current all-in transportation cost including payments, insurance, fuel, maintenance, parking, and registration, then calculate savings from realistic alternatives like one car instead of two, less expensive vehicle, or eliminating car ownership entirely if feasible.

Third, calculate your current monthly food spending across groceries and restaurants based on actual transactions over the past three months rather than estimates, then calculate potential savings from cooking at home more, meal planning to reduce waste, and strategic grocery shopping that minimizes convenience purchases. Fourth, total the potential savings from realistic optimizations across all three categories to see exactly how much monthly and annual savings you could capture through big-win changes rather than small daily deprivations. Fifth, choose the one big win that requires the least disruption or sacrifice relative to savings, then commit to implementing it within the next thirty to ninety days rather than indefinitely planning without action.

Monthly Spending Optimization Checklist:

Create a systematic process for reviewing and optimizing your spending monthly, catching lifestyle inflation and unnecessary expenses before they become entrenched habits that feel permanent and necessary. First, export your previous month's spending from your bank and credit card accounts, categorizing every transaction into housing, transportation, food, entertainment, shopping, subscriptions, and other relevant categories. Second, identify the three largest expenses within each category and evaluate whether each provided value proportional to its cost or whether cheaper alternatives could provide similar benefit.

Third, look for recurring charges you didn't consciously use that month like subscriptions, memberships, or services you're paying for out of habit rather than active value, canceling immediately anything you haven't used in the past thirty days. Fourth, identify any impulse purchases over fifty dollars and evaluate whether you'd make the same purchase again knowing what you know now after owning the item for a few weeks, learning from regrettable purchases to prevent similar mistakes next month. Fifth, calculate your savings rate as percentage of income and evaluate whether it increased, decreased, or stayed flat compared to prior months, investigating any decreases to understand whether they represent lifestyle inflation that needs reversing or one-time unusual expenses that won't recur.

House Hacking Scenarios:

Evaluate whether house hacking makes sense for your situation by calculating specific scenarios with real numbers from your local market rather than abstract theorizing about whether you'd be willing to have roommates or tenants. First, research duplex, triplex, or fourplex properties in areas where you'd be willing to live, identifying typical purchase prices and rental rates for similar units. Second, calculate the all-in monthly cost of purchasing and living in one unit including mortgage principal and interest, property taxes, insurance, maintenance, and vacancy reserves, then subtract the rental income from other units to determine your net housing cost or potential positive cash flow.

Third, compare this net cost to your current housing expense to see whether house hacking would save money even before accounting for equity building through tenants paying down your mortgage and property appreciation. Fourth, honestly assess whether you'd be willing to accept the responsibilities and lifestyle trade-offs of being a live-in landlord in exchange for the financial benefits, considering that you'd be dealing with tenant issues, maintenance problems, and reduced privacy compared to traditional home ownership or renting. Fifth, if the numbers work and you're willing to accept the trade-offs, begin serious planning for house hacking within the next six to eighteen months including improving credit if needed, saving for down payment, and researching local landlord laws and requirements.

Anti-Lifestyle Inflation Commitment Contract:

Create formal commitments about how you'll handle income increases going forward to prevent lifestyle inflation from automatically consuming raises and bonuses, giving your future self clear rules rather than relying on in-the-moment discipline. First, commit to automatically increasing retirement contributions or investment account transfers by at least fifty percent of any raise, programming this increase to happen automatically with HR or your bank before the first larger paycheck arrives and spending can absorb the increase. Second, commit to waiting at least ninety days before making any new recurring spending commitments after receiving a raise, preventing the immediate lifestyle inflation that often occurs when increased income feels like permission to upgrade everything.

Third, establish clear rules about which lifestyle improvements are worth paying for with raises and which aren't, based on your values and genuine impact on wellbeing rather than social expectations or vague feelings that you deserve to spend more because you're earning more. Fourth, schedule annual reviews of all recurring expenses to identify lifestyle creep that happened despite intentions to avoid it, canceling or downgrading anything that's no longer providing proportional value. Fifth, track your savings rate as percentage of income as your primary financial metric rather than absolute savings or income numbers, ensuring that higher income actually improves your financial trajectory rather than just funding higher spending that leaves you equally stressed at every income level.

Strategic frugality is not about deprivation or penny-pinching that makes your life miserable in service of some distant abstract goal; it's about intelligently allocating resources to what actually matters while ruthlessly cutting waste that provides minimal benefit. When you focus on the big wins of housing, transportation, and food while avoiding lifestyle inflation, you can build wealth quickly while maintaining or even improving quality of life because you're spending intentionally on what matters rather than diffusing resources across countless things that don't. The wealth you build through strategic spending comes not from suffering or sacrifice but from clarity about your actual values and willingness to ignore social pressure to spend money proving your success to people who don't actually care about you.

9

Tax Optimization - Keep More of What You Earn

Section 1: Understanding the Tax Game

Taxes represent one of the largest expenses most people will pay over their lifetimes, often exceeding what they spend on housing or any other single category, yet the vast majority of people put more effort into saving fifty dollars on groceries than saving thousands on taxes because tax planning feels complicated, intimidating, or like something only accountants and wealthy people need to think about. This passive approach to taxes costs average earners tens or hundreds of thousands of dollars over their careers through missed deductions, sub optimal account choices, and failure to understand basic tax strategies that could legally and ethically reduce their tax burden substantially while accelerating wealth building.

The fundamental truth about taxes is that the tax code is essentially a series of incentives designed to encourage specific behaviors like retirement saving, home ownership, business creation, charitable giving, and education, and people who engage in these incentive behaviors pay dramatically less tax than people who ignore the incentives and just earn and spend without strategic planning. Understanding this principle transforms taxes from a mysterious burden you passively accept into a game with clear rules where informed players can legally reduce their obligations by tens of thousands of dollars while building wealth faster through tax-advantaged accounts and strategies. You're not cheating or being unethical by minimizing taxes through legal strategies; you're simply understanding and using the system as designed.

How taxes actually work in a progressive system confuses most people who believe oversimplified narratives about tax brackets without understanding marginal rates, leading them to reject raises or income opportunities out of mistaken fear that earning more will somehow leave them with less money after taxes. The reality of progressive taxation is that you never lose money by earning more because only the dollars above each bracket threshold are taxed at the higher rate, not your entire income. Understanding this prevents the common error of declining opportunities because you've heard someone say "I'll be in a higher tax bracket" as if that's automatically bad when it actually just means you're earning enough that the last dollars you earn are taxed at slightly higher rates while all the previous dollars remain taxed at the lower rates.

Marginal versus effective tax rates represent the critical distinction that most people don't understand, leading to massive confusion about what they actually pay in taxes. Your marginal rate is the tax percentage applied to your last dollar of income, the rate that applies to additional earning if you get a raise or bonus. Your effective rate is your total tax divided by your total income, representing what percentage you actually pay overall after accounting for the progressive bracket structure. These numbers are often dramatically different, with someone in the twenty-two percent marginal bracket typically having an effective rate of perhaps twelve to fifteen percent, meaning they keep eighty-five to eighty-eight cents of every dollar they earn despite being "in the twenty-two percent bracket."

For example, someone earning seventy thousand dollars in 2024 as a single filer falls in the twenty-two percent marginal bracket, leading them to say they're "in the twenty-two percent tax bracket" and perhaps believing they pay twenty-two percent of their income in federal taxes. In reality, the first eleven thousand dollars is taxed at ten percent, the next thirty-three thousand is taxed at twelve percent, and only the remaining twenty-six thousand is taxed at twenty-two percent, resulting in total federal tax of approximately ten thousand seven hundred dollars, an effective rate of just fifteen percent. This person keeps eighty-five cents of every dollar earned on average, and if they got a five thousand dollar raise, they'd keep about thirty-nine hundred after federal taxes, not making less money despite entering a higher bracket as they might fear.

Tax bracket misconceptions prevent people from maximizing income opportunities, accepting raises, or converting to higher-paid contract work because they've somehow concluded that earning more will make them worse off financially. This fundamentally misunderstands progressive taxation and costs people enormous amounts of lifetime income because they're artificially limiting their earning potential based on false beliefs about how taxes work. Earning more always leaves you with more money after taxes in a progressive system; the only question is how much more you keep, with marginal rates determining what percentage of additional income you retain rather than whether additional income is worthwhile.

The only scenario where earning more could theoretically hurt you is through benefit cliffs where government assistance programs cut off sharply at certain income thresholds, potentially creating situations where earning slightly more makes you ineligible for benefits worth more than the income increase. These cliffs exist for programs like Medicaid, subsidized housing, SNAP benefits, and various other assistance programs, creating genuine disincentives to income increases for people near the cutoff thresholds. But these situations are specific to means-tested benefits and don't apply to most working people, and even for people facing benefit cliffs, the long-term wealth-building advantage of higher income usually outweighs the temporary loss of benefits if you're strategic about planning the transition.

Why tax planning matters for wealth extends far beyond just minimizing your annual tax bill, though that alone creates substantial value through keeping more of what you earn. Strategic tax planning accelerates wealth building by directing more money toward investment accounts where it compounds tax-free or tax-deferred for decades, using the tax code's incentives to amplify your saving and investing behavior. The difference between someone who understands tax-advantaged accounts and maxes them out versus someone who pays full taxes on all income and then invests what's left can easily exceed hundreds of thousands of dollars over a career, making tax optimization one of the highest-return activities for your time and attention.

Consider two people each earning one hundred thousand dollars annually and saving twenty percent toward retirement. Person A contributes twenty thousand to a traditional 401k, reducing taxable income to eighty thousand and paying perhaps fourteen thousand in federal taxes based on a fifteen percent effective rate, with the full twenty thousand growing tax-deferred in the retirement account. Person B doesn't use retirement accounts and pays perhaps nineteen thousand in taxes on the full one hundred thousand, then invests the after-tax twenty thousand in a taxable brokerage account where dividends and capital gains are taxed annually. After thirty years, Person A has accumulated significantly more wealth both because they invested more each year thanks to the tax deduction and because the investments grew without the drag of annual taxes, potentially creating a difference of several hundred thousand dollars in final wealth from these tax planning differences alone.

Common misconceptions about taxes include believing that deductions directly reduce your tax bill dollar-for-dollar when they actually reduce taxable income which then reduces taxes by your marginal rate, thinking that tax refunds are bonuses rather than interest-free loans you gave the government through over withholding, assuming that tax planning is only for the wealthy when many strategies benefit middle-income earners more on a percentage basis, and believing that any legal tax reduction is somehow unethical when the entire tax code is designed to incentivize specific behaviors through preferential treatment. Understanding these misconceptions helps you approach tax planning rationally rather than emotionally, optimizing legally and ethically rather than either overpaying out of ignorance or underpaying through aggressive positions that create audit risk.

Section 2: Tax-Advantaged Accounts

Tax-advantaged retirement accounts represent the single most powerful tax optimization strategy for most people, allowing you to either defer taxes on contributions and growth until retirement or pay taxes now and enjoy tax-free growth and withdrawals forever depending on which account type you choose. These accounts are the government's primary tool for incentivizing retirement savings, and the tax benefits are so substantial that maximizing contributions should be your first priority before almost any other investment strategy unless you have high-interest debt or inadequate emergency funds. Understanding the different account types and their benefits helps you deploy your limited savings dollars optimally to minimize lifetime taxes while building retirement wealth.

The 401k and employer match represents free money that should be your absolute first investing priority, capturing the immediate hundred percent return from employer matching before considering any other investment or even aggressive debt payoff beyond minimums. Most employers offer to match your 401k contributions up to some percentage of salary, commonly three to six percent, meaning if you contribute that percentage they'll add an equal amount of free money to your account. This match is immediate return before any market gains, making it the best guaranteed return available anywhere in investing and absolute financial malpractice to decline by failing to contribute enough to capture the full match.

The mechanics are straightforward: if your employer matches fifty percent of contributions up to six percent of salary, you need to contribute six percent to get the full three percent match. On a seventy thousand dollar salary, contributing six percent means forty-two hundred dollars annually from your paycheck plus twenty-one hundred from employer match, giving you sixty-three hundred total retirement saving from just forty-two hundred of your money. That twenty-one hundred match is fifty percent immediate return on your forty-two hundred contribution before accounting for any market growth, a return that no other investment can match and makes failing to contribute enough to get full match equivalent to leaving thousands of dollars of compensation on the table annually.

Beyond the match, 401k contributions up to the annual limit provide tax deferral that reduces your current taxes while allowing investments to grow without annual tax drag. For 2024, the employee contribution limit is twenty-three thousand dollars with an additional seventy-five hundred for people over fifty, amounts that high earners should maximize before investing in taxable accounts due to the substantial tax savings. Contributing twenty-three thousand to a traditional 401k saves someone in the twenty-two percent marginal bracket about five thousand sixty dollars in federal taxes immediately, money they can invest rather than sending to the government, while the investments grow tax-deferred until retirement when they're hopefully in lower brackets and can withdraw more tax-efficiently.

The traditional versus Roth choice for retirement accounts represents one of the most important tax planning decisions you'll make, determining whether you pay taxes now at current rates on contributions but enjoy tax-free growth and withdrawals, or defer taxes now but pay them later on all withdrawals including growth. Traditional accounts make sense when you expect to be in a lower tax bracket in retirement than you are now, allowing you to deduct contributions at your current higher marginal rate and pay taxes on withdrawals at lower retirement rates. Roth accounts make sense when you expect taxes to be higher in retirement than now, either because you're currently in low brackets early in your career or because you believe tax rates will increase generally over the decades before you retire.

For most people in their twenties and thirties who are in relatively low tax brackets, Roth contributions make more sense because they're paying perhaps twelve to twenty-two percent taxes now to enjoy completely tax-free growth and withdrawals in retirement when they're likely in higher brackets and tax rates might be higher generally. For people in their peak earning years in high brackets, traditional contributions often make more sense because the immediate deduction at twenty-four to thirty-seven percent marginal rates provides substantial current tax savings, and they can potentially convert some of those traditional savings to Roth during lower-income years in early retirement before taking Social Security. There's no universally right answer, and many people benefit from having both traditional and Roth accounts to create tax diversification in retirement.

IRA contribution limits and strategies extend the tax-advantaged space beyond employer plans, allowing you to contribute up to seven thousand dollars annually (as of 2024) to traditional or Roth IRAs regardless of whether you have a 401k, though income limits may restrict destructibility of traditional contributions or Roth eligibility for high earners. For people without employer plans or who have maximized 401k contributions and still want to save more in tax-advantaged space, IRAs provide additional capacity though the contribution limits are much lower than 401k limits. The real power of IRAs often comes through the backdoor Roth conversion strategy for high earners who can't contribute to Roth IRAs directly due to income limits.

The backdoor Roth IRA works by making non-deductible contributions to a traditional IRA, which anyone can do regardless of income, then immediately converting those contributions to a Roth IRA which has no income restrictions for conversions. This multi-step process achieves the same result as direct Roth IRA contributions for high earners who are above the income limits for regular Roth contributions, allowing them to get money into Roth accounts where it grows tax-free forever. The conversion is tax-free because you didn't take a deduction for the traditional IRA contribution, making this a legal workaround to income restrictions that tax lawyers confirm is legitimate if done correctly with proper accounting.

HSA triple tax advantage makes health savings accounts possibly the most powerful tax-advantaged account available, though they're only accessible to people with high-deductible health insurance plans. HSAs offer tax deductions on contributions like traditional retirement accounts, tax-free growth like Roth accounts, and tax-free withdrawals for medical expenses unlike both traditional and Roth which tax either contributions or withdrawals. This triple tax advantage means money you contribute to HSAs is never taxed as long as you use it for qualifying medical expenses either now or in the future, creating a uniquely powerful savings vehicle.

The optimal HSA strategy for people who can afford it is contributing the maximum annually, investing the full balance rather than spending it on current medical expenses, paying current medical expenses from taxable accounts while saving receipts, and letting the HSA balance grow tax-free for decades until retirement when you can reimburse yourself for all those saved receipts tax-free or use the funds for the substantial medical expenses most people incur in retirement. For 2024, the contribution limits are four thousand one hundred fifty for individuals and eighty-four hundred for families, with an additional thousand catch-up contribution for people over fifty-five. Someone who maxes out family HSA contributions and invests for thirty years could easily accumulate several hundred thousand dollars of completely tax-free money for medical expenses, creating a powerful supplement to regular retirement accounts.

529 plans for education provide tax-free growth for college savings though contributions aren't federally deductible, with many states offering deductions or credits for contributions to their state's plan. The value of 529s comes primarily from tax-free growth over the fifteen to twenty years between opening accounts when children are young and spending the money on college, allowing moderate monthly contributions to compound into substantial college funds without paying taxes on gains. Someone contributing three hundred dollars monthly to a 529 from a child's birth until age eighteen would accumulate over ninety thousand dollars at seven percent returns, all of which can be withdrawn tax-free for qualified education expenses including tuition, fees, books, and room and board.

The downsides of 529s include limited flexibility since money must be used for qualified education expenses or face taxes and penalties on earnings, though recent law changes allow up to ten thousand dollars for K-12 tuition and up to thirty-five thousand in lifetime transfers to Roth IRAs for beneficiaries. These flexibility improvements make 529s less risky than they used to be for parents worried about over-funding or children not attending college, though they still require more planning than general investment accounts. For parents certain their children will attend college and looking for tax-advantaged ways to save for that expense, 529s provide meaningful benefits through tax-free growth that can amount to thousands or tens of thousands in tax savings over eighteen years.

Section 3: Deductions and Credits You're Missing

Standard versus itemized deductions represent the first decision in optimizing your tax return, determining whether you take the fixed standard deduction amount that requires no documentation or itemize specific deductible expenses that exceed the standard deduction. For 2024, the standard deduction is fourteen thousand six hundred for single filers and twenty-nine thousand two hundred for married filing jointly, amounts that most people don't exceed through itemized deductions and therefore benefit more from taking the standard deduction without tracking receipts or maintaining documentation. However, people with large mortgages, substantial state and local taxes, major medical expenses, or large charitable contributions can often itemize for larger total deductions.

The Tax Cuts and Jobs Act of 2017 nearly doubled standard deductions while capping or eliminating many itemized deductions, making itemization beneficial for far fewer people than before. Previously, perhaps thirty percent of taxpayers itemized; now fewer than fifteen percent benefit from itemization, with the standard deduction being optimal for most middle-class families. This doesn't mean ignoring itemized deductions entirely, but it does mean that many people who religiously tracked deductions pre-2017 are wasting time documenting expenses that won't exceed their standard deduction and therefore provide no tax benefit.

Home office deduction allows people who are self-employed or own businesses to deduct expenses for the portion of their home used exclusively and regularly for business, potentially saving thousands annually in taxes for people with dedicated home office spaces. The deduction can be calculated using the simplified method of five dollars per square foot up to three hundred square feet, or the regular method that deducts actual expenses like mortgage interest, insurance, utilities, and depreciation prorated by the percentage of home used for business. A home office representing ten percent of a home's square footage could deduct ten percent of mortgage interest, property taxes, utilities, insurance, and repairs, potentially creating deductions of several thousand dollars annually.

The critical requirement that trips up many people is that the space must be used exclusively and regularly for business, meaning a spare bedroom that's primarily an office but also contains a guest bed or workout equipment doesn't fully qualify. The IRS scrutinizes home office deductions because of widespread abuse, making it crucial to follow rules precisely and maintain documentation showing exclusive business use. For people who qualify, the deduction provides meaningful tax savings that can amount to twenty to thirty percent of home office expenses depending on marginal tax rates, making proper setup and documentation worthwhile for legitimate home-based businesses.

Business expense deductions for self-employed individuals and business owners represent one of the most powerful tax reduction strategies, allowing deduction of virtually any ordinary and necessary expense for operating your business from advertising and marketing to travel and meals to software and equipment. These deductions reduce your business income before calculating self-employment taxes and income taxes, providing potentially huge savings for people running profitable businesses. A consultant earning eighty thousand dollars gross might have twenty thousand in deductible business expenses including home office, vehicle, technology, marketing, professional development, and insurance, reducing taxable income to sixty thousand and saving perhaps six thousand to eight thousand in taxes depending on rates and deductions.

Understanding what qualifies as deductible business expenses requires knowing the IRS standard of ordinary and necessary, meaning expenses that are common and accepted in your industry and appropriate and helpful for your business. This is deliberately broad, allowing deductions for many expenses employees cannot deduct including vehicles used primarily for business, meals with clients or for business travel, continuing education and professional development, professional licenses and memberships, business insurance, and marketing costs. The key is maintaining documentation showing business purpose and keeping business and personal expenses clearly separated to demonstrate that deducted expenses were genuinely for business rather than personal use.

Travel and meal deductions for business purposes provide valuable tax savings for people who travel for work or regularly meet clients for meals, though recent law changes have limited meal deductions and created confusion about what remains deductible. As of current law, business meals are fifty percent deductible when they have a clear business purpose like meeting a client or business associate to discuss work, while entertainment expenses are generally no longer deductible after Tax Cuts and Jobs Act changes. Travel expenses including airfare, hotels, and fifty percent of meals remain fully deductible when traveling away from your tax home for business purposes, potentially creating substantial deductions for consultants, salespeople, or business owners with significant travel.

The documentation requirements for travel and meals are strict, requiring contemporaneous records showing the business purpose, people involved, topics discussed, and amounts spent. Many people lose deductions during audits because they can't demonstrate business purpose beyond vague claims, while people who maintain detailed calendars and notes can substantiate substantial deductions that save thousands in taxes. For people with significant business travel or meals, proper documentation practices pay for themselves many times over through preserved deductions.

Tax credits for education, children, and energy differ from deductions in that they reduce tax owed dollar-for-dollar rather than just reducing taxable income, making them potentially much more valuable than deductions especially for people in lower tax brackets. The American Opportunity Tax Credit provides up to twenty-five hundred dollars per eligible student for the first four years of college, directly reducing tax by the full credit amount rather than just reducing taxable income by tuition paid. The Child Tax Credit provides two thousand dollars per child under seventeen, with fourteen hundred potentially refundable even if you don't owe taxes, creating substantial value for families with multiple children.

Energy credits for residential clean energy installations like solar panels, geothermal heat pumps, or energy-efficient windows and doors can reduce taxes by thirty percent of installation costs up to specific limits, potentially creating credits of thousands or tens of thousands of dollars for major home energy improvements. Someone installing a forty thousand dollar solar panel system could claim a twelve thousand dollar tax credit, directly reducing taxes owed by that full amount rather than just deducting the expense. These credits are designed to incentivize specific behaviors like education investment or clean energy adoption, making them extremely valuable for people undertaking these activities anyway who should ensure they're claiming all available credits.

Section 4: Advanced Tax Strategies

Tax-loss harvesting in investment accounts provides one of the few ways to reduce taxes on investment gains without actually selling winners, using realized losses to offset realized gains while maintaining similar market exposure. The strategy involves selling investments that have declined in value to realize losses for tax purposes, then immediately purchasing similar but not identical investments to maintain desired market exposure while capturing the tax benefit. The realized losses offset capital gains dollar-for-dollar, and up to three thousand dollars of excess losses can offset ordinary income annually with additional losses carrying forward to future years.

The execution requires understanding wash sale rules that prohibit selling a security at a loss and repurchasing the same or substantially identical security within thirty days before or after the sale, which would disallow the loss. To avoid this, you sell the losing position and immediately buy a similar but not identical investment, such as selling one S&P 500 index fund and buying a different S&P 500 index fund or a total market index fund. This maintains similar market exposure while capturing the tax loss, creating value through tax savings without changing investment strategy or taking time out of the market. Over many years of tax-loss harvesting in taxable accounts, the accumulated tax savings can add twenty to thirty basis points of annual return through tax alpha, meaningfully enhancing after-tax investment returns.

Charitable giving strategies go far beyond just writing checks to charities, using techniques like donating appreciated stock, bunching contributions into alternating years, using donor-advised funds for multi-year contributions, and qualified charitable distributions from IRAs for retirees. The basic principle is that charitable contributions are deductible when itemizing, but the standard deduction is high enough that many people don't itemize annually even with charitable giving. Bunching solves this by making two years of contributions in one year to exceed the standard deduction and itemize that year, then taking the standard deduction the following year when you don't donate, creating larger total deductions over the two-year period than annual giving would provide.

Donating appreciated stock or other assets that have gained value provides additional tax benefits beyond just deducting the contribution because you avoid capital gains tax on the appreciation while still deducting the full fair market value. If you bought stock for one thousand dollars that's now worth five thousand and you're in the twenty-four percent tax bracket, donating the stock allows you to deduct five thousand (saving twelve hundred dollars in taxes) while avoiding capital gains tax on the four thousand gain (saving potentially six hundred dollars in federal capital gains tax). The combined tax benefit of eighteen hundred dollars from donating five thousand of stock is much larger than the twelve hundred you'd save from donating five thousand cash, making appreciated securities the preferred donation method for people with taxable investment accounts.

Donor-advised funds provide even more flexibility for charitable giving by allowing you to make large contributions in high-income years to get immediate tax deductions, invest the funds to grow tax-free, and recommend grants to charities over many subsequent years. This strategy works well for people with irregular income like business owners or sales people who want to make large deductible contributions in high-earning years but distribute the actual charitable giving over time. You could contribute fifty thousand to a donor-advised fund in a year where you sold a business or had unusually high income, immediately deducting the full fifty thousand, then grant five thousand annually to charities over ten years while the balance grows in the fund tax-free.

Real estate tax benefits make property ownership one of the most tax-advantaged investments available, combining deductible expenses, depreciation that shelters income while property appreciates, and preferential capital gains treatment when selling. Rental property owners can deduct mortgage interest, property taxes, insurance, maintenance, property management fees, and depreciation which is a non-cash deduction that reduces taxable income without actual cash outflow. Depreciation allows you to deduct roughly three point six percent of the property's value annually for twenty-seven point five years even while the property is likely appreciating in value, creating a magical situation where you're deducting losses while building equity through appreciation.

The depreciation deduction shelters rental income from taxation, often creating situations where rental properties show tax losses despite generating positive cash flow, and those losses can offset other passive income or up to twenty-five thousand dollars of ordinary income for active participants in rental real estate meeting specific criteria. When you eventually sell appreciated rental property, you can defer all capital gains tax indefinitely through 1031 exchanges into new properties, allowing real estate investors to build portfolios worth millions while deferring all taxes until they finally sell without exchanging, if ever. This combination of deductions, depreciation, and tax-deferred exchanges makes real estate uniquely tax-favored compared to stocks or other investments.

When to hire a CPA versus DIY tax preparation depends on the complexity of your tax situation, the value of your time, your comfort with tax software, and whether you have business income, rental properties, stock compensation, or other complications that benefit from professional expertise. Simple W-2 employee returns with standard deductions can easily be handled through software like Turbo Tax or FreeTaxUSA for minimal cost, with the software asking questions and selecting appropriate forms automatically. More complex situations involving business income, multiple states, rental properties, stock options, large capital gains, or high income generally benefit from CPA assistance both for ensuring correct filing and for proactive tax planning that saves more than the CPA fees.

The value of a good CPA goes beyond just preparing your annual return to include tax planning throughout the year, advice on major financial decisions with tax implications, representation if you're audited, and strategic guidance on business structure, retirement contributions, and other moves that reduce taxes. Someone paying two thousand dollars for CPA services who saves five thousand through strategies they wouldn't have known about or implemented alone is getting tremendous value beyond just the compliance service of return preparation. The decision should be based on the complexity of your situation and the likely value of professional advice, with simple situations handled DIY and complex situations justified CPA expense as an investment in better outcomes.

Actionable Takeaways

Tax optimization transforms from passive acceptance of whatever you owe to active strategic management that keeps thousands more of your earnings annually, but only if you move from theoretical knowledge to actual implementation of the strategies covered in this chapter. The gap between people who pay minimum legal tax and people who overpay through ignorance or inaction is pure execution, taking time to understand your options, set up tax-advantaged accounts, track deductible expenses, and make strategic decisions throughout the year rather than just accepting whatever tax bill arrives in April. This month you need to take concrete actions that will reduce your taxes this year and in future years.

Tax Optimization Checklist:

Create a systematic plan for implementing every applicable tax strategy from this chapter, starting with the highest-value easiest-to-implement strategies before moving to more complex optimizations. First, ensure you're contributing enough to your 401k to capture full employer match, which is free money you're leaving on the table if you're not maxing the match. Second, calculate whether you should contribute to traditional or Roth retirement accounts based on your current tax bracket and expected retirement bracket, adjusting contributions accordingly. Third, open and fund an HSA if you have a high-deductible health plan, maximizing contributions and investing the balance rather than spending it on current medical expenses.

Fourth, review whether you have enough itemized deductions to exceed your standard deduction, stopping the time-consuming tracking of expenses if you're nowhere close to exceeding the standard amount. Fifth, if you're self-employed or own a business, ensure you're tracking all deductible business expenses and deducting everything legally allowable including home office, vehicle, equipment, and professional development. Sixth, implement tax-loss harvesting in taxable investment accounts by identifying positions with losses and selling them to offset gains or up to three thousand of ordinary income, immediately replacing with similar but not identical investments to maintain market exposure.

Deduction Tracking System:

Set up systems now for tracking deductible expenses throughout the year rather than scrambling to reconstruct spending from memory when preparing taxes, ensuring you capture all available deductions instead of losing thousands through poor documentation. First, create a simple spreadsheet or use expense tracking software to categorize business expenses, charitable contributions, medical expenses, and other potentially deductible items as you incur them throughout the year. Second, maintain a dedicated folder for receipts and documentation, either digital or physical, organized by category so you have support for claimed deductions if questioned.

Third, if you're self-employed or run a business, separate business and personal finances completely with dedicated business bank accounts and credit cards, making it trivial to identify deductible expenses versus commingled personal spending. Fourth, for vehicle deductions, maintain a mileage log showing business versus personal use either through apps that track automatically or manual tracking in a logbook, as vehicle deductions are frequently challenged and require solid documentation. Fifth, review your tracking system monthly rather than annually to catch missing documentation or categorization errors while memory is fresh, correcting issues throughout the year rather than discovering at tax time that six months of records are missing or inadequate.

Annual Tax Planning Calendar:

Create a schedule of tax planning activities throughout the year rather than only thinking about taxes during filing season, turning tax optimization into an ongoing process that maximizes savings through strategic timing of income and deductions. In January, review the previous year's return to identify missed opportunities or strategies to implement for the current year, and adjust withholding if you had a large refund or owed significantly since optimal withholding means breaking even rather than providing interest-free loans to the government. In March, make prior-year IRA contributions before the tax filing deadline, maximizing retirement account contributions for the previous year if you have funds available.

In June, review year-to-date income and estimate annual earnings to determine whether you'll exceed Roth IRA income limits or need to implement backdoor Roth conversions, and assess whether bunching charitable contributions or other itemized deductions makes sense for the current year. In

September, plan and execute any tax-loss harvesting if you have positions with losses that could offset gains or ordinary income, and review retirement account contributions to ensure you're on track to maximize annual limits. In November, finalize any charitable giving, business expense purchases, or retirement contributions needed before year-end to optimize the current year's taxes, and consider tax-gain harvesting to realize capital gains in low-income years.

Business Structure Evaluation:

If you're self-employed or running a side business, evaluate whether your current business structure is optimal for tax purposes or whether incorporating as an S-Corp or LLC could save thousands annually through reduced self-employment taxes and additional deduction opportunities. First, calculate your annual business profit after expenses to determine if S-Corp status might save money, generally making sense when profits exceed sixty to eighty thousand annually depending on your situation. Second, understand that S-Corps allow you to split income between reasonable salary subject to payroll taxes and distributions not subject to self-employment tax, potentially saving three thousand to ten thousand annually in self-employment taxes on profits above the reasonable salary threshold.

Third, consult with a CPA about whether your specific situation justifies the additional complexity and cost of S-Corp status including payroll processing, additional tax filings, and compliance requirements. Fourth, if incorporating makes sense, work with a business attorney or formation service to properly establish the entity, obtain an EIN, and set up compliant processes for payroll and distributions. Fifth, maintain rigorous separation between personal and business finances if operating as a corporation or LLC, as commingling funds can pierce the corporate veil and eliminate liability protection and tax benefits that justified the entity formation.

Tax optimization is not about aggressive positions or questionable deductions that create audit risk; it's about understanding the legal incentives built into the tax code and using them fully to minimize your tax burden while building wealth through tax-advantaged accounts and strategic deductions. The tax code is deliberately designed to encourage specific behaviors through preferential treatment, and people who understand and use these incentives legally and ethically pay dramatically less tax than people who ignorantly overpay through passive acceptance of their tax situation. Implement the strategies in this chapter systematically and you'll keep thousands more of your earnings annually, money that compounds into tens or hundreds of thousands over decades of optimized tax planning.

10

Investing 101 - Making Your Money Work for You

Section 1: Why Investing is Non-Negotiable

The decision to invest or not invest isn't really a decision at all if you understand basic mathematics and the reality of inflation, because keeping money in cash or savings accounts guarantees you're losing purchasing power every year while investing gives you the only realistic chance of building wealth that actually grows faster than the cost of living. This isn't theoretical or debatable; it's mathematical reality that separates people who build meaningful wealth from people who work their entire lives and die with almost nothing to show for decades of labor. Understanding why investing is absolutely essential rather than just a good idea motivates the commitment required to learn investing basics and overcome the fear or inertia that keeps millions of people stuck in cash while inflation slowly destroys their savings.

Inflation represents the silent wealth destroyer that most people dramatically underestimate because they focus on their growing account balances without considering whether those balances buy more or less than they used to.

Historical inflation averages approximately three percent annually, though recent years have seen periods of much higher inflation that devastate people living on fixed incomes or holding cash. Three percent annual inflation means your money loses half its purchasing power every twenty-three years, so ten thousand dollars today will buy what five thousand buys in twenty-three years if you just hold cash earning nothing. This wealth destruction happens invisibly and gradually, making it psychologically easier to ignore than dramatic losses from bad investments, but the long-term impact is devastating for people who avoid investing out of fear.

High-yield savings accounts earning four to five percent might seem like they beat inflation and preserve purchasing power, but after taxes on interest income your real return drops to perhaps three percent for someone in the twenty-two percent bracket, barely keeping pace with inflation in good years and losing purchasing power during high inflation periods. Holding emergency funds and short-term savings in high-yield accounts makes sense because that money needs to be safe and accessible, but holding all your wealth in cash or savings accounts guarantees you'll never build meaningful wealth regardless of how much you earn or save. The opportunity cost of not investing compounds over decades into differences of hundreds of thousands or millions of dollars between people who invested consistently and people who saved cash.

The power of compound interest represents the most important wealth-building principle in existence, transforming small consistent investments into enormous wealth over decades through exponential growth that most people struggle to grasp intuitively. Albert Einstein allegedly called compound interest the eighth wonder of the world, noting that those who understand it earn it while those who don't pay it. The mathematics are simple but profound: money invested at ten percent annually doubles every seven point two years, meaning one dollar invested at age twenty-five becomes sixteen dollars by age seventy-five through compound growth alone without adding another cent. This exponential growth explains why starting young matters so much and why consistent investing over decades creates wealth that saving alone never can.

The difference between someone who starts investing at age twenty-five versus thirty-five is not just the ten years of contributions but the compound growth on those early contributions over the full investing timeline. Someone investing five hundred dollars monthly starting at twenty-five accumulates approximately one point nine million by sixty-five at ten percent returns, while someone starting at thirty-five with the same monthly investment accumulates only seven hundred thousand, less than half despite only a ten-year delay in starting. This happens because the contributions made between twenty-five and thirty-five, just sixty thousand in total, grow to one point two million over forty years through compounding, accounting for most of the difference between the two scenarios. Starting early is the single most valuable investing decision you can make.

Time in the market versus timing the market separates successful investors who build wealth from unsuccessful ones who chase returns and panic sell during downturns, destroying wealth through emotional decision-making rather than patient systematic investing. Market timing means trying to predict when markets will rise or fall and making buy-sell decisions based on those predictions, a strategy that sounds reasonable but has been proven repeatedly to under perform simple buy-and-hold investing for the vast majority of people who attempt it. Professional money managers with teams of analysts and sophisticated models mostly fail to beat market indexes through timing, so individual investors trying to time the market without professional resources are almost certain to under perform.

The data on timing versus time in market is conclusive: missing just the ten best days in the stock market over a twenty-year period reduces returns by approximately half compared to staying fully invested, and those best days often occur during volatile periods when people are tempted to sell, meaning the investors who panic and move to cash during uncertainty miss the very days that generate most of the market's long-term returns. Someone who invested ten thousand dollars in the S&P 500 in 1998 and stayed fully invested through all the volatility including the 2000 tech crash, 2008 financial crisis, and 2020 pandemic would have over seventy thousand by 2024, while someone who missed the ten best days would have only thirty-five thousand, half the return despite being invested ninety-nine percent of the time.

Real wealth comes from ownership, not saving, because wealth is built through assets that generate returns or appreciate in value rather than through accumulated cash that loses purchasing power and generates no meaningful growth. Employees who save diligently but never invest might accumulate six-figure account balances over decades, but they're not building real wealth because that cash generates minimal returns and gets slowly eroded by inflation. Investors who own stocks, real estate, or businesses watch their assets appreciate and generate income while they sleep, building wealth through ownership of productive assets rather than just through saving portions of earned income.

This ownership principle explains why the wealth gap continues widening between investors and savers, with asset owners seeing their wealth grow exponentially through compound returns and appreciation while savers see their purchasing power decline or barely keep pace with inflation despite working and saving consistently. The path to wealth isn't working harder or earning more necessarily, though those help; it's converting earned income into ownership of appreciating assets as quickly and consistently as possible, then letting time and compound returns do the heavy lifting while you continue adding to those assets through ongoing contributions. Every dollar you save without investing is a dollar that will never work for you and will slowly lose value through inflation.

Section 2: Investment Basics Demystified

Stocks represent ownership shares in publicly traded companies, giving you a proportional claim on the company's assets and earnings along with the right to benefit from the company's growth through stock price appreciation and potentially dividend payments. When you buy Apple stock, you literally become a tiny owner of Apple with rights to a proportional share of their profits, and if Apple grows and becomes more profitable over time, your ownership stake becomes more valuable. This ownership characteristic differentiates stocks from bonds or savings accounts where you're lending money for fixed returns rather than owning pieces of businesses that can grow without limits.

The value of stocks fluctuates constantly based on investor perceptions of company prospects, economic conditions, industry trends, and countless other factors both rational and emotional, creating the volatility that makes stocks risky in short timeframes but historically rewarding over long periods. A stock that drops twenty percent in a month hasn't actually lost twenty percent of the company's value in most cases; investors have just decided temporarily that they're willing to pay twenty percent less for ownership of that company based on new information or changing sentiment. This volatility scares many people away from stock investing, but it's the price you pay for the higher long-term returns that stocks provide compared to safer investments like bonds or cash.

Historical stock market returns average approximately ten percent annually over long periods like decades or centuries, though any particular year might see returns ranging from negative forty percent in severe crashes to positive forty percent in boom years. This average return of ten percent is what makes stocks the most important wealth-building tool for most people, as no other commonly available investment offers similar risk-adjusted returns over multi-decade periods. Someone investing consistently in broad stock market indexes over thirty or forty years can expect to achieve returns close to this historical average, while someone chasing individual stocks or trying to time the market will likely under perform significantly.

Bonds represent loans you make to governments or corporations in exchange for fixed interest payments and eventual return of your principal, providing more stable and predictable returns than stocks but with much lower growth potential over long periods. When you buy a ten-year Treasury bond, you're lending money to the U.S. government which promises to pay you interest semi-annually and return your principal in ten years, with almost zero risk of default since the government can print money if needed. Corporate bonds carry more risk than government bonds since companies can default, but they pay higher interest rates to compensate for that risk, giving bond investors a range of risk-return options from essentially risk-free government bonds to speculative high-yield corporate bonds.

The role of bonds in investment portfolios is providing stability and predictable income while reducing overall volatility compared to all-stock portfolios, making them most important for people near retirement who need to preserve capital and can't afford to wait out multi-year stock market declines. Young investors with decades until retirement should hold mostly or entirely stocks because they have time to recover from crashes and benefit from the higher long-term returns stocks provide, while retirees might hold fifty to seventy percent bonds to ensure they can meet spending needs without being forced to sell stocks during downturns. The traditional rule suggesting your bond allocation should equal your age is overly conservative for most people given longer life expectancy and lower bond yields, but the principle of increasing bond allocation as retirement approaches remains sound.

Mutual funds and ETFs provide diversification by pooling money from many investors to purchase baskets of stocks or bonds rather than requiring individual investors to buy hundreds of individual securities themselves. A total stock market mutual fund might hold three thousand different stocks representing the entire U.S. stock market, giving investors who own shares of the fund instant diversification across all those companies through a single purchase. This diversification is crucial for managing risk because it ensures that no single company's failure or industry's decline destroys your portfolio, spreading risk across many companies and industries so that winners offset losers.

The difference between mutual funds and ETFs is mostly technical rather than fundamental, with both offering similar diversification benefits but differing in how they trade and their expense structures. Mutual funds are priced once daily after markets close and transactions occur directly with the fund company, while ETFs trade throughout the day on exchanges like individual stocks with prices fluctuating based on supply and demand. ETFs typically have lower expense ratios than comparable mutual funds because they're passively managed and have lower operational costs, making them preferable for most investors who don't need specific mutual fund features like automatic investment plans or the ability to trade fractional shares.

Index funds represent a specific category of mutual funds or ETFs that track market indexes like the S&P 500 or total stock market rather than trying to beat the market through active stock selection. An S&P 500 index fund simply buys all five hundred companies in that index weighted by their market capitalization, providing investors with returns that match the index minus tiny fees rather than trying to outperform through active management. This passive approach has been proven to beat the vast majority of actively managed funds over long periods because active management fees typically exceed whatever additional returns active managers generate through stock picking, making index funds the best choice for most investors.

The case for index fund investing was definitively proven by Warren Buffet's famous bet where he wagered one million dollars that an S&P 500 index fund would outperform a selection of hedge funds over ten years, and after a decade the index fund had more than doubled the returns of the best hedge fund and crushed the average return of all five selected funds. This happened despite the hedge funds being run by brilliant professional investors with research teams and advanced strategies, because their high fees and trading costs destroyed enough returns that simple low-cost index fund investing won easily. If professional investors can't beat index funds consistently after fees, individual investors have essentially no chance and should stop trying.

Real estate investment basics include both direct ownership of rental properties and indirect ownership through REITs or real estate crowdfunding platforms, each with distinct advantages and disadvantages for different investor situations. Direct property ownership provides maximum control and potentially higher returns through rental income, tax benefits like depreciation, and property appreciation, but requires substantial capital for down payments, active management of tenants and maintenance, and acceptance of concentration risk from holding large portions of wealth in one or a few properties. REITs allow real estate investing with minimal capital through stock-like shares of companies that own and manage properties, providing diversification and liquidity that direct ownership cannot match.

The decision between direct property investment and REITs depends primarily on your available capital, time and willingness to manage properties, local market opportunities, and whether you want real estate to be an active business or a passive investment component of a diversified portfolio. Someone with fifty thousand dollars, limited time, and no interest in property management should probably buy REITs through their brokerage account and enjoy passive real estate exposure. Someone with two hundred thousand saved, time to manage properties, and strong local market knowledge might build substantial wealth through direct property ownership and leverage. There's no universally right answer, and many wealthy people use both approaches depending on opportunity and circumstance.

Section 3: Understanding Risk and Diversification

Risk tolerance assessment represents the crucial first step in building an investment portfolio because your ability to stick with an investment strategy through market volatility matters more than having the theoretically optimal allocation on paper. If you build an aggressive all-stock portfolio because the numbers say it's optimal for young investors but you panic sell during the first twenty percent market decline, you've destroyed wealth and would have been better off with a more conservative allocation you could actually maintain. Understanding your true risk tolerance requires honest self-assessment about how you'd react to seeing your portfolio drop twenty, thirty, or even fifty percent during severe market crashes.

The distinction between risk tolerance and risk capacity matters for understanding appropriate portfolio construction, as tolerance is psychological while capacity is financial. Risk tolerance is your emotional ability to watch your portfolio decline without panicking and selling at losses; risk capacity is your financial ability to absorb losses without impacting your life or goals. A young person with forty years until retirement has extremely high risk capacity because they can wait out any market decline and have decades for recovery, but they might have low risk tolerance if market volatility causes anxiety and sleep loss. Ideally your investment allocation matches both your capacity and tolerance, but in conflicts tolerance often matters more because you can't benefit from high capacity if you panic sell before recovery.

Testing your risk tolerance honestly requires imagining specific scenarios rather than abstract questions about willingness to accept volatility for higher returns. If you have one hundred thousand invested and the market crashes thirty percent, how would you feel watching your balance drop to seventy thousand? Would you panic sell to stop the bleeding, hold your position and hope for recovery, or excitedly buy more at lower prices? Your honest answer to this scenario reveals your true tolerance better than any questionnaire asking whether you're "willing to accept short-term volatility for long-term growth" because everyone says yes to that question in good times but many people fail the test when actual volatility arrives.

Diversification means spreading investments across different asset classes, industries, geographic regions, and individual securities so that no single investment or category dominates your portfolio and exposes you to catastrophic losses. The principle "don't put all your eggs in one basket" is probably the most important investing wisdom for most people, because concentrated positions in single stocks or industries have destroyed countless fortunes while properly diversified portfolios weather even severe downturns and eventually recover. Someone with their entire portfolio in tech stocks learned this painfully during the 2000 tech crash when tech-heavy portfolios lost seventy to eighty percent while diversified portfolios lost much less.

The mathematics of diversification show that adding stocks to a portfolio reduces volatility dramatically at first but the benefits diminish as you add more positions, with most benefits captured by holding twenty to thirty individual stocks from different industries. Beyond thirty or so stocks, additional diversification provides minimal volatility reduction while increasing complexity and transaction costs, which is why most investors should simply own total market index funds holding thousands of stocks rather than trying to build optimally diversified portfolios of individual stocks. The total market fund provides maximum diversification with zero effort and minimal cost, capturing the full benefits of diversification without the work or expertise required to select and manage individual positions.

Risk versus reward relationship means investments with higher potential returns inherently carry higher risk of losses, and there's no secret strategy that provides high returns without corresponding risk despite what scammers selling investment courses might claim. Stocks provide higher long-term returns than bonds because they're riskier with more volatility and potential for loss; bonds provide lower returns than stocks because they're safer with more predictable outcomes. Any investment promising stock-like returns with bond-like safety is either a fraud or involves risks the promoter isn't disclosing, because market efficiency ensures that genuine opportunities for high return with low risk get bid up until they no longer offer that attractive combination.

Understanding this risk-reward trade-off prevents chasing supposedly safe high-return investments that turn out to be frauds like Bernie Madoff's Ponzi scheme that claimed consistent double-digit returns with minimal risk and collapsed destroying billions in investor wealth. Legitimate investments distribute along a clear risk-reward spectrum from virtually risk-free Treasury bonds earning minimal returns to highly volatile stocks or speculative investments that might generate huge returns or catastrophic losses. The optimal portfolio for most people combines multiple asset classes at different points on this spectrum to create risk-adjusted returns matching their goals and tolerance rather than trying to maximize returns without regard to risk.

Age-based asset allocation suggests younger investors should hold mostly stocks for maximum growth potential while gradually shifting toward bonds as retirement approaches to preserve accumulated wealth and reduce volatility. The traditional rule of holding bond allocation equal to your age, meaning a thirty-year-old holds thirty percent bonds and a sixty-year-old holds sixty percent, provides a starting framework though it's probably too conservative for most people given longer retirements and lower bond yields. A more aggressive approach might be one hundred minus your age in stocks, meaning a thirty-year-old holds seventy percent stocks and a sixty-year-old holds forty percent, providing more growth potential while still adding stability as retirement nears.

The logic behind increasing bond allocation with age is straightforward: younger people have time to recover from market crashes and benefit from higher long-term stock returns, while people near or in retirement might need to sell investments soon for living expenses and can't afford to wait out multi-year recovery periods. A thirty-year-old who sees their portfolio drop forty percent in a crash can simply hold the positions and wait for recovery over the next five to ten years while continuing to add money at lower prices, actually benefiting from the crash through lower purchase prices. A sixty-five-year-old who sees the same decline might be forced to sell at losses to fund retirement spending, permanently locking in losses rather than waiting for recovery.

Section 4: Getting Started with Any Amount

Micro-investing apps and platforms have democratized investing by allowing people to start with minimal amounts rather than requiring thousands of dollars to open accounts, eliminating the historical barrier that kept many people from investing until later in their careers when they'd accumulated substantial savings. Apps like Acorns, Stash, or M1 Finance allow investing with as little as five dollars and offer automatic investing features that round up purchases to the nearest dollar and invest the difference, making investing nearly effortless for people who struggle with the discipline to manually transfer money to investment accounts.

The benefits of micro-investing apps include eliminating barriers to starting, automating investment contributions through round-ups or scheduled transfers, and providing simple user interfaces that make investing less intimidating than traditional brokerage platforms. These benefits particularly help young people or those new to investing who might delay starting because the process seems complicated or they feel they don't have enough money to begin. Getting started with any amount, even tiny contributions, is infinitely better than waiting until you have more money because the habit formation and time in market matter more than contribution size in the early stages.

The downsides of micro-investing apps include higher fees as a percentage of small balances compared to traditional brokerages, limited investment options compared to full-service brokerages, and account minimums or monthly fees that can eat into returns when balances are small. Someone with a one hundred dollar balance paying one dollar monthly in fees is paying twelve percent annually in costs, completely destroying any returns they might earn. For this reason, micro-investing apps are best as starting points to build the investing habit and initial balances, with the goal of eventually moving to lower-cost platforms once balances grow to thousands of dollars where the fee impact becomes minimal.

Brokerage account setup at major providers like Fidelity, Vanguard, or Charles Schwab requires just minutes online and provides access to thousands of investment options including stocks, bonds, mutual funds, and ETFs with no account minimums or monthly fees for basic accounts. These traditional brokerages have eliminated most of the friction and costs that historically kept small investors away, now offering commission-free stock and ETF trading, no account minimums for standard accounts, and user-friendly mobile apps comparable to micro-investing platforms. For people who can start with at least a few hundred dollars, opening accounts at these established brokerages provides better long-term value than micro-investing apps.

The account opening process involves providing personal information including name, address, Social Security number, employment information, and bank account details for funding transfers. The brokerage needs this information for regulatory compliance and to verify your identity, not for any nefarious purpose, and all major brokerages are heavily regulated financial institutions that protect customer information and assets through SIPC insurance covering up to five hundred thousand dollars per account. Once your account is approved, usually within one business day, you can link your bank account and transfer money to begin investing immediately.

Rob-advisors versus self-directed investing presents a choice between automated portfolio management based on questionnaires about your goals and risk tolerance versus manually selecting and managing your own investments. Rob-advisors like Betterment or Wealth front ask about your age, income, goals, and risk tolerance, then build diversified portfolios of ETFs matching your profile and automatically re balance as markets move or your situation changes. This automation is perfect for people who want professional-quality portfolio management without paying human advisor fees or spending time researching investments and managing re balancing.

The cost of rob-advisors typically runs about zero point two-five percent of assets under management annually, far less than human financial advisors charging one percent or more but still meaningful over decades on large balances. Someone with five hundred thousand in a rob-advisor pays about twelve hundred fifty dollars annually in fees compared to perhaps one hundred dollars in fees for a self-managed portfolio of similar low-cost index funds. This fee difference matters less for beginners with small balances where twelve hundred fifty dollars of fees is far in the future, but eventually self-directed investing in simple index funds becomes more cost-effective than rob-advisor management.

Dollar-cost averaging strategy means investing fixed amounts at regular intervals regardless of market conditions rather than trying to time entry points or investing lump sums all at once. This approach is optimal for people investing monthly from paychecks because they don't have lump sums to invest anyway, but it's also psychologically beneficial for reducing the anxiety about whether you're buying at the wrong time. When you invest five hundred dollars monthly into an S&P 500 index fund on the first of every month regardless of whether the market is high or low, you automatically buy more shares when prices are low and fewer shares when prices are high, averaging your purchase price over time.

The mathematics show that lump sum investing immediately beats dollar-cost averaging in the long run roughly two-thirds of the time because markets trend upward more than downward over long periods, making delay costly through missed gains. However, the psychological benefits of dollar-cost averaging for reducing anxiety and preventing paralysis often outweigh the mathematical suboptimality, especially for people who might delay investing for months or years trying to time the perfect entry point. Better to start investing through dollar-cost averaging immediately than to wait indefinitely for the perfect moment that never arrives, because time in market beats timing the market consistently.

Actionable Takeaways

Investing transforms from abstract concept to actual wealth building only when you open accounts, transfer money, and purchase investments that will grow over decades while you continue adding to them consistently. The gap between people who build substantial wealth through investing and people who die with minimal assets despite earning good incomes is simply taking action rather than endlessly planning or waiting for perfect conditions. This week you need to open investment accounts if you don't have them and make your first investments if you've been sitting in cash, overcoming inertia and fear through action that gets easier with each subsequent contribution.

Risk Tolerance Quiz:

Complete this honest self-assessment of your true risk tolerance to guide appropriate asset allocation rather than building a portfolio you can't psychologically maintain through volatility. First, imagine your portfolio losing ten percent in a month and viscerally feel how that would affect your stress, sleep, and confidence in your investing strategy, rating your discomfort on a scale of one to ten. Second, imagine a thirty percent decline over six months with financial media screaming about crashes and friends talking about moving to cash, rating how likely you'd be to panic sell versus hold or buy more.

Third, consider your historical behavior during the 2008 financial crisis,

2020 pandemic crash, or other volatile periods if you were investing then, honestly assessing whether you held your positions, panic sold near the bottom, or confidently bought more at lower prices. Fourth, reflect on whether you lose sleep or feel significant anxiety when your portfolio declines or whether you view volatility as expected and unimportant to long-term outcomes. Fifth, based on these honest assessments, determine whether you can psychologically handle aggressive all-stock portfolios, need more conservative mixed allocations, or require very conservative bond-heavy portfolios to maintain discipline and avoid panic selling.

Investment Platform Comparison Chart:

Systematically evaluate different investing platforms to choose the one that best matches your current situation and investing approach rather than just using whatever platform a friend recommends or appears first in search results. Create a comparison chart with platforms across the top including major brokerages like Fidelity, Vanguard, and Schwab, micro-investing apps like Acorns or Stash, and rob-advisors like Betterment or Wealth front. Down the left side, list evaluation criteria including account minimums, fees and expense ratios, available investments, ease of use, customer service, educational resources, and automatic investing features.

Research each platform across these dimensions, filling in the chart with specific details rather than vague impressions, then score each platform on the factors most important to your situation. If you're starting with small amounts, prioritize low minimums and automatic features over breadth of investment options you won't use anyway. If you have substantial savings to invest, prioritize low fees and broad investment selection over beginner features. If you want completely hands-off management, robo-advisors score highest despite higher fees compared to self-directed approaches. Choose the platform that scores best for your specific situation rather than the objectively "best" platform.

First Investment Checklist:

Create a specific plan for making your first investments this week rather than indefinitely planning without action, breaking the intimidating process into concrete sequential steps that make getting started achievable. First, open accounts at your chosen platform by completing the online application with required personal and financial information, linking your bank account, and funding with an initial transfer of whatever amount you can afford to invest. Second, while waiting for funds to settle, research and select your initial investments using simple broad index funds like total market or S&P 500 funds rather than trying to pick individual stocks or build complex portfolios.

Third, once your funds are available, execute your first purchase of the simple index fund you've selected, accepting that this first purchase will feel uncomfortable but is necessary to begin the investing habit. Fourth, set up automatic monthly contributions from your checking account to your investment account on the same schedule as your paycheck, ensuring that investing happens consistently rather than only when you remember or feel motivated. Fifth, commit to not checking your account balance more than monthly at most, avoiding the anxiety and potential poor decisions that come from obsessive monitoring of short-term volatility.

Investment Policy Statement Template:

Create a written investment plan that codifies your strategy, rules, and commitments to prevent emotional decisions during market volatility when fear or greed might otherwise override your rational long-term plan. Your investment policy statement should include specific sections: investment goals with target amounts and timelines, risk tolerance assessment and appropriate asset allocation based on that tolerance, specific investments you'll hold and why you selected them, rules for re balancing when allocations drift from targets, and commitments about what you will NOT do like panic sell during crashes or chase performance into hot sectors.

Write specific scenarios and your planned responses: "If my portfolio declines twenty percent, I will hold all positions and continue regular contributions, buying at lower prices" and "If friends or media suggest selling due to market conditions, I will review this policy statement and remember my long-term plan rather than reacting emotionally." Having these commitments written when you're rational and calm provides crucial guidance when markets are volatile and emotional responses might otherwise destroy wealth through poor timing. Review and update this policy statement annually but resist the urge to change fundamental strategy based on short-term performance or market conditions.

The transformation from non-investor to investor happens through a single decision followed by a series of simple actions that become habitual over weeks and months, building the confidence and discipline that separates wealthy people from those who work their entire lives without building lasting wealth. Your first investment might be just one hundred dollars in a total market index fund, a tiny amount that feels almost meaningless, but it represents the beginning of a wealth-building process that compounds over decades into financial independence if you maintain consistency and resist the temptation to abandon your plan during inevitable volatility. Every wealthy investor started exactly where you are now, with small initial investments and uncertainty about whether they were doing it right, but they maintained discipline through market cycles and built wealth through time and compounding rather than brilliance or luck.

11

Building Your Wealth Portfolio - The Long Game

Section 1: Retirement Accounts First

The priority order for deploying your savings and investment dollars matters enormously because different account types provide different tax benefits, employer contributions, and withdrawal flexibility that make some accounts dramatically more valuable than others for the same dollar invested. Most people approach investing haphazardly, opening whatever account type they hear about first or splitting money evenly across different options without understanding the mathematical differences in outcomes based on account selection. Understanding the optimal order for funding different account types can increase your retirement wealth by tens or hundreds of thousands of dollars through better tax treatment and captured employer matching that people who invest randomly miss completely.

Maximizing employer 401k match represents the absolute first priority for anyone with access to employer retirement plans, capturing the guaranteed immediate hundred percent return that employer matching provides before considering any other investment or even paying off moderate-interest debt.

If your employer matches fifty percent of contributions up to six percent of salary, you're getting a guaranteed fifty percent return on that six percent before any market gains, a return that no other investment can match and makes not contributing enough to get full match equivalent to declining free money. This match is part of your compensation package that you're leaving on the table if you don't contribute enough to capture it fully.

The mathematics are straightforward and compelling: someone earning seventy thousand dollars with a fifty percent match up to six percent who contributes the full six percent gets forty-two hundred from their paycheck plus twenty-one hundred from employer match, totaling sixty-three hundred in their 401k from just forty-two hundred of their money. That twenty-one hundred match is fifty percent immediate return, and even if the market returns zero that year, you've still made fifty percent on your contribution through the match alone. Over a career, capturing full match versus not contributing generates differences of hundreds of thousands of dollars in retirement wealth, making this the single highest-return financial decision most employees can make.

Beyond the match, additional 401k contributions up to the annual limit provide tax deferral that reduces current taxes while allowing investments to grow without annual tax drag, making continued 401k contributions valuable even after capturing full employer match. The decision about how much additional 401k money to contribute beyond the match depends on your tax bracket, whether you have high-interest debt, whether you've maximized other tax-advantaged options, and your income level. High earners in top tax brackets saving thousands immediately on each dollar of 401k contribution should generally max out 401k contributions before taxable investing, while lower earners might benefit more from Roth IRA contributions or paying off debt.

The 401k contribution limit for 2024 is twenty-three thousand dollars in employee deferrals with an additional seventy-five hundred catch-up contribution for people over fifty, limits that high earners should maximize to capture maximum tax deferral and tax-free growth. Someone in the twenty-four percent marginal tax bracket contributing twenty-three thousand saves fifty-five hundred twenty dollars in current federal taxes while that twenty-three thousand grows tax-deferred potentially for decades, making the 401k contribution far more valuable than investing the same amount in a taxable account where you'd first pay taxes on the income then pay taxes annually on investment gains.

IRA contribution limits and strategies provide additional tax-advantaged space beyond employer plans, allowing up to seven thousand dollars annually in traditional or Roth IRA contributions depending on income and whether you're covered by an employer plan. For people without employer plans, IRAs represent their primary retirement savings vehicle and should be maximized before taxable investing. For people who've captured full 401k match and are deciding where to contribute next, Roth IRAs often provide better value than additional traditional 401k contributions for people in moderate tax brackets who expect higher retirement tax rates.

The Roth IRA versus traditional 401k decision for contributions beyond employer match depends primarily on your current versus expected future tax rates, with Roth making sense when current rates are lower than expected retirement rates and traditional making sense in the reverse. Someone in their twenties earning fifty thousand in the twelve percent tax bracket should probably prioritize Roth IRA contributions over additional traditional 401k because they're paying just twelve percent tax now to enjoy completely tax-free growth and withdrawals in retirement when they'll likely be in higher brackets. Someone in their peak earning years in the thirty-two percent bracket might benefit more from traditional 401k contributions that save thirty-two percent in current taxes even though withdrawals will be taxed.

The backdoor Roth IRA strategy allows high earners above Roth income limits to still get money into Roth IRAs through a multi-step process of making non-deductible traditional IRA contributions then immediately converting them to Roth, achieving the same result as direct Roth contributions despite being above income limits. This strategy requires careful accounting and assumes you don't have existing traditional IRA balances that would trigger pro-rata taxation on conversions, but for high earners with no traditional IRA balances it provides valuable access to Roth benefits that would otherwise be unavailable due to income restrictions.

Asset allocation by life stage means your mix of stocks, bonds, and other assets should shift over time as you age and your financial situation changes, generally becoming more conservative as retirement approaches and you have less time to recover from market crashes. Young investors in their twenties and thirties should hold primarily or entirely stocks because they have decades until retirement to wait out crashes and benefit from stocks' higher long-term returns, making short-term volatility irrelevant to their outcomes. Middle-aged investors in their forties and fifties might begin adding bond allocations of twenty to forty percent to reduce portfolio volatility while still maintaining growth through majority stock holdings.

Investors approaching retirement in their sixties should generally hold forty to sixty percent in bonds to preserve accumulated wealth and reduce the sequence-of-returns risk where crashes early in retirement can devastate withdrawal sustainability. The exact allocation at any age depends on personal risk tolerance, retirement timeline, other income sources like pensions or rental properties, and withdrawal needs, but the general principle of gradually reducing stock exposure as retirement approaches helps ensure you don't experience devastating losses right when you need to begin withdrawing funds for living expenses.

Section 2: Index Fund Investing Strategy

Total market index funds represent the simple, low-cost, diversified foundation that should form the core of most investors' portfolios, providing exposure to thousands of companies across the entire market rather than requiring stock picking or active management decisions. A total stock market index fund like Vanguard's VT SAX or Fidelity's FZROX holds essentially every publicly traded U.S. company weighted by market capitalization, giving you ownership of everything from massive corporations like Apple and Microsoft to tiny companies you've never heard of. This complete diversification ensures you capture market returns without the risk that poor selection of individual stocks or sectors under performs.

The beauty of total market index funds is that they require zero investing expertise or ongoing management while delivering returns that beat the vast majority of professionally managed funds after accounting for fees. You're not trying to identify which stocks or sectors will outperform; you're simply owning the entire market and accepting whatever returns the market delivers, which historically averages about ten percent annually over long periods. This approach feels boring compared to exciting stock picking or sector bets, but boring consistently beats exciting in investing because excitement usually means volatility and under performance while boring index fund investing quietly builds wealth through consistent market returns.

S&P 500 index funds provide similar benefits to total market funds but hold only the five hundred largest U.S. companies rather than the entire market, capturing about eighty percent of total U.S. market capitalization in just five hundred holdings. The performance difference between total market and S&P 500 funds is minimal over long periods because large companies dominate total market fund returns anyway, making either option perfectly fine as core portfolio holdings. Some investors prefer total market for slightly better diversification including small companies; others prefer S&P 500 for the focus on established large companies with proven business models.

The practical reality is that the choice between total market and S&P 500 index funds matters far less than the choice to invest in index funds at all versus trying to pick winners or holding cash, because both options provide excellent low-cost diversified exposure to U.S. stock market returns. Someone agonizing over which to choose is optimizing the wrong variable; just pick one based on whichever has lower expense ratios at your brokerage and move on to the more important questions of how much to invest and maintaining discipline through market cycles.

International diversification through international index funds adds exposure to companies headquartered outside the U.S., providing true global diversification rather than just owning U.S. companies that happen to do business internationally. A total international stock fund holds thousands of companies across developed and emerging markets in Europe, Asia, and other regions, allowing your portfolio to benefit if international stocks outperform U.S. stocks or providing some hedge if U.S. markets under perform. The percentage of your stock allocation to dedicate to international stocks is debated endlessly, with recommendations ranging from twenty to fifty percent depending on who you ask.

A reasonable approach is holding twenty to thirty percent of your stock allocation in international funds, providing meaningful international exposure without over-concentrating in markets that might under perform U.S. stocks for extended periods as they have for the past decade-plus. Someone with one hundred thousand in stocks might hold seventy thousand in total U.S. market funds and thirty thousand in total international funds, capturing both U.S. and international returns while maintaining U.S. home bias that reflects both the size of U.S. markets and the tendency for domestic stocks to better match domestic spending needs in retirement.

Bond index funds for stability become increasingly important as retirement approaches and you need to reduce portfolio volatility to avoid being forced to sell stocks during downturns to fund living expenses. A total bond market index fund holds thousands of U.S. government and corporate bonds with varying maturities, providing stable returns of perhaps three to five percent annually with much less volatility than stocks. Bonds serve as portfolio ballast, holding value or even appreciating during stock market crashes when investors flee to safety, preventing the psychological trauma and poor decision-making that often occurs when all-stock portfolios decline thirty to fifty percent.

The role of bonds is not maximizing returns but rather reducing volatility to levels you can psychologically tolerate while providing funds to sell for re balancing or withdrawals when stocks crash, allowing you to maintain your investment strategy rather than panic selling everything. Someone with fifty percent bonds won't see their portfolio drop as much during crashes because the bond portion stays relatively stable, making it easier to stay invested and wait for stock recovery rather than selling everything at the bottom. This volatility reduction is worth accepting the lower long-term returns bonds provide compared to stocks.

The three-fund portfolio represents the ultimate simple yet effective investment strategy, holding just total U.S. stock market fund, total international stock fund, and total bond market fund in proportions matching your desired asset allocation. Someone thirty years old might hold sixty percent U.S. stocks, thirty percent international stocks, and ten percent bonds, while someone sixty might hold forty percent U.S. stocks, twenty percent international stocks, and forty percent bonds. This simple three-fund approach provides comprehensive global diversification across thousands of securities with minimal cost and zero ongoing management beyond annual re balancing.

The genius of the three-fund portfolio is that it's sophisticated in its simplicity, capturing all the benefits of diversification and low-cost indexing while eliminating the complexity, costs, and under performance that come from trying to add value through active management or complex strategies. Investors with three-fund portfolios often outperform investors with ten or twenty different funds because they avoid the over-trading, sector chasing, and high fees that destroy returns despite feeling more active and engaged. Sometimes the best investment decision is the one that lets you set up your portfolio once and then largely ignore it while focusing on earning more money and contributing consistently.

Section 3: Re balancing and Staying the Course

Annual portfolio re balancing maintains your target asset allocation as different investments grow at different rates, selling winners and buying losers to bring the portfolio back to intended proportions. If you target sixty percent stocks and forty percent bonds but stock growth has shifted your portfolio to seventy percent stocks and thirty percent bonds, re balancing means selling enough stocks and buying bonds to restore the sixty-forty split. This forces the valuable discipline of selling high and buying low that most investors struggle to do emotionally, systematically taking some profits from assets that have run up while adding to assets that have declined.

The benefits of re balancing include maintaining intended risk levels rather than allowing portfolios to drift toward higher stock allocations and risk during bull markets, forcing systematic profit-taking from winners before bubbles burst, and providing a mechanical process that removes emotion from buy-sell decisions. Portfolios left to drift without re balancing often become dangerously stock-heavy after extended bull markets right before major crashes, maximizing losses during downturns because the high stock allocation happened to coincide with overvalued markets. Regular re balancing prevents this drift and forces some defensive positioning.

The frequency of re balancing represents a trade-off between maintaining target allocations and avoiding excessive trading costs or taxes in taxable accounts, with annual re balancing providing a reasonable balance for most investors. Some research suggests re balancing only when allocations drift beyond certain thresholds like five or ten percentage points provides similar risk control with less frequent trading, while others prefer calendar-based re balancing quarterly or annually for simplicity. The perfect re balancing frequency probably doesn't exist and the differences in long-term outcomes are minimal, making any consistent approach far better than no re balancing strategy.

Tax considerations in taxable accounts make re balancing more complex because selling winners triggers capital gains taxes that reduce the benefit of re balancing, suggesting that re balancing should primarily occur in tax-advantaged retirement accounts where sales don't trigger taxes. For portfolios split between taxable and retirement accounts, execute re balancing trades in retirement accounts when possible to avoid tax consequences, only re balancing taxable accounts when allocations drift significantly or when you have losses to harvest that can offset gains from re balancing sales.

Avoiding emotional investing means maintaining your investment strategy through market volatility rather than buying when euphoric and selling when terrified, the pattern that destroys more wealth than almost any other investor behavior. The market cycle of greed during bull markets and fear during crashes creates predictable emotional responses that lead to terrible decisions: buying stocks near market tops when everyone is excited and prices are highest, then selling near bottoms when panic is maximum and prices are lowest. This buy-high-sell-low approach guarantees under performance and destroyed wealth despite feeling rational in the moment when fear or greed overwhelm logic.

Understanding that these emotional impulses are normal and expected rather than signs of weakness helps you prepare strategies to override them when they arrive. Every investor feels fear during thirty to fifty percent crashes and questions whether this time really is different and stocks will never recover; every investor feels the pull to chase hot sectors or stocks during bubbles when it seems like everyone else is getting rich while you're stuck in boring index funds. The difference between successful investors and unsuccessful ones isn't whether they feel these emotions but whether they act on them or override them through commitment to long-term strategy.

Market crashes and when to buy more represent some of the most psychologically difficult but financially rewarding moments in investing, when prices are drastically reduced and future returns from new investments are likely to be excellent yet fear makes buying feel impossible. Every market crash eventually recovered to new highs, making crashes incredible buying opportunities for investors with cash and courage to invest when fear is maximum. Someone who invested heavily during the 2008 financial crisis, 2020 pandemic crash, or other major downturns earned spectacular returns over the following recovery period, but doing so required overriding overwhelming fear that markets might never recover.

The mechanical approach to crash investing is maintaining your regular investment contributions regardless of market conditions, automatically buying more shares when prices are low without requiring you to emotionally commit to investing during crashes. Dollar-cost averaging through crashes means your regular five hundred or one thousand dollar monthly investment buys more shares during the downturn, lowering your average cost per share and positioning you for outsize gains during recovery. If you can muster the courage to actually increase contributions during crashes rather than just maintaining them, the long-term wealth impact can be enormous.

The danger of panic selling cannot be overstated because selling during crashes locks in losses permanently rather than allowing time for recovery that has happened after every historical crash. The investor who sold everything during the 2008 financial crisis when the market had dropped fifty percent missed the subsequent recovery that not only recouped all losses but delivered substantial additional gains to people who stayed invested. That panic selling transformed a temporary paper loss that would have recovered into a permanent realized loss, destroying wealth that patient investors kept and grew.

Preventing panic selling requires planning and commitment during calm markets when you're rational rather than trying to make decisions during crashes when fear distorts thinking. Write down now, while markets are calm, how you'll respond when your portfolio drops twenty, thirty, or fifty percent: you'll maintain regular contributions, you'll not check balances more than monthly, you'll reread your investment policy statement reminding yourself why you chose your strategy, and you'll absolutely not sell unless your fundamental life situation has changed requiring the funds for genuine emergencies. This per-commitment while rational helps override the temptation to abandon your plan when emotional during actual crashes.

Section 4: Advanced Portfolio Strategies

Target-date funds provide automatic age-appropriate asset allocation and re balancing through single-fund solutions that shift from aggressive to conservative as you approach the target retirement date, making them ideal for investors who want simplicity and don't want to manage allocations themselves. A 2050 target-date fund designed for people retiring around 2050 holds primarily stocks now since retirement is distant, then gradually shifts toward bonds over the next twenty-five years until reaching a conservative allocation at the target date. This automatic re balancing and allocation shift happens without any action required from investors beyond holding the fund.

The benefits of target-date funds include complete simplicity requiring just one fund purchase and no ongoing management, automatic re balancing saving you from having to sell winners and buy losers annually, and guaranteed age-appropriate allocation preventing the common mistake of being too aggressive near retirement or too conservative when young. These benefits are substantial for people who might otherwise make poor allocation decisions, fail to re balance consistently, or simply want investing to be completely hands-off so they can focus on earning and contributing rather than managing portfolios.

The downsides of target-date funds include slightly higher expense ratios than building your own three-fund portfolio, typically fifteen to thirty basis points versus five to ten basis points for separate index funds, though this cost difference is minimal on small balances. More significantly, target-date funds use one-size-fits-all glide paths that might not match your specific risk tolerance or retirement plans, potentially being too conservative for people with high risk tolerance or too aggressive for conservative investors. They also limit tax optimization strategies like asset location since you can't control where stocks versus bonds are held across taxable and retirement accounts.

For most investors, especially those just starting or those who know they won't maintain disciplined re balancing, target-date funds represent excellent solutions that deliver solid results through simplicity despite slightly higher costs compared to self-managed portfolios. The investor who holds a target-date fund and never touches it will likely outperform the investor who tries to actively manage a three-fund portfolio but makes emotional decisions during volatility or fails to re balance consistently. Simplicity often beats complexity in investing because it reduces opportunities for harmful decisions.

Tax-loss harvesting in taxable accounts provides one of the few legal ways to reduce taxes without changing investment strategy, selling positions with losses to offset capital gains while immediately replacing them with similar investments to maintain market exposure. The mechanics involve monitoring your taxable account for positions trading below purchase price, selling those positions to realize losses for tax purposes, and immediately buying similar but not identical investments to maintain desired asset allocation. The losses offset any capital gains dollar-for-dollar, and excess losses beyond gains can offset up to three thousand dollars of ordinary income annually with remaining losses carrying forward indefinitely.

The implementation requires understanding wash sale rules prohibiting repurchasing the same or substantially identical security within thirty days before or after selling at a loss, which would disallow the loss deduction. To avoid wash sales, sell the losing position and immediately buy a similar but different fund, such as selling a Vanguard S&P 500 fund and buying a Fidelity S&P 500 fund, or selling an S&P 500 fund and buying a total market fund. The similarity maintains your desired market exposure while the difference avoids wash sale rules, capturing the tax benefit without changing investment strategy.

The value of tax-loss harvesting accumulates over decades of implementation, with studies showing it can add twenty to fifty basis points of annual after-tax returns through tax savings that wouldn't exist without systematic harvesting. Someone with five hundred thousand in taxable accounts might harvest five to ten thousand in losses annually during volatile years, saving one thousand to two thousand in taxes depending on their capital gains rate. Over thirty years of consistent harvesting, these tax savings compound into substantial differences in after-tax wealth that justify the modest complexity of maintaining a harvesting strategy.

Asset location strategy means intentionally placing different asset types in taxable versus tax-advantaged accounts to minimize lifetime taxes, typically holding tax-inefficient assets like bonds and REITs in retirement accounts while holding tax-efficient assets like stock index funds in taxable accounts. Bonds generate ordinary income taxed at higher rates than long-term capital gains, making them more valuable in tax-deferred accounts where that income isn't taxed annually. Stock index funds generate minimal taxable distributions and mostly grow through unrealized capital gains that aren't taxed until sold, making them relatively tax-efficient in taxable accounts.

The implementation might mean holding your entire bond allocation in 401k or IRA accounts while holding only stock funds in taxable accounts, even if this means your taxable account is entirely stocks while your retirement accounts hold all bonds and some stocks. This allocation might seem odd when looking at individual accounts but makes sense when viewing your entire portfolio across all accounts as a unified whole, optimizing after-tax returns through strategic placement of assets where they're taxed most favorably.

The benefits of optimal asset location can add twenty to forty basis points of annual return through tax savings on a typical portfolio split across taxable and retirement accounts, not as large as the benefit from stock versus bond allocation decisions but meaningful over decades. Someone with half their portfolio in taxable accounts and half in 401k/IRA accounts might save two thousand to five thousand dollars annually through optimal asset location on a million-dollar portfolio, money that compounds into hundreds of thousands over retirement accumulation and withdrawal phases.

Actionable Takeaways

Building a wealth portfolio transforms from theoretical knowledge into actual growing assets only through specific actions that deploy your savings into appropriate accounts and investments following the priority order and strategies covered in this chapter. Most people who read about investing either never start, invest haphazardly without strategy, or abandon their plans during first market downturn, behaviors that guarantee they'll never build the wealth that consistent strategic investing creates. This month you need to implement the specific portfolio building blocks that will grow into financial independence over decades of consistent contributions and disciplined adherence to your strategy.

Portfolio Allocation Calculator by Age:

Determine your specific target asset allocation based on your current age, risk tolerance, and retirement timeline rather than using generic rules that might not fit your situation. Start with a baseline of holding your age in bonds with the remainder in stocks, then adjust based on risk tolerance: aggressive investors might subtract ten to twenty years from their age before calculating bond percentage, while conservative investors might add ten years. For someone forty years old with average tolerance, this suggests forty percent bonds and sixty percent stocks as a starting point.

Next, divide your stock allocation between U.S. and international funds, using twenty to thirty percent of stock allocation for international as a general guideline. A forty-year-old with sixty percent stocks and forty percent bonds might hold forty percent U.S. stocks, twenty percent international stocks, and forty percent bonds. Write down these specific percentages as your target allocation, then calculate dollar amounts for each category based on your current portfolio value and determine what purchases will move you toward these targets.

Re balancing Schedule and Checklist:

Create a systematic annual re balancing process that maintains your target allocation without requiring constant monitoring or emotional decision-making throughout the year. Choose a specific annual date for re balancing, perhaps your birthday or January first, and calendar the event with reminders so you actually follow through each year rather than forgetting. On your re balancing date, calculate your current allocation by dividing each asset category's value by total portfolio value, comparing these current percentages to your targets to identify which assets are overweight and need trimming versus underweight and need additions.

Execute re balancing trades in tax-advantaged accounts when possible to avoid triggering capital gains taxes, selling overweight assets and buying underweight assets to restore target allocations. In taxable accounts, consider whether rebalancing is urgent enough to justify taxes or whether you can achieve rebalancing through directing new contributions to underweight assets rather than selling winners. Document your rebalancing activity including dates, amounts, and reasoning so you have a record of maintaining discipline through your investment timeline.

Investment Policy Statement:

Write a comprehensive investment policy statement that codifies your long-term strategy, target allocations, re balancing rules, and behavioral commitments to provide guidance during periods when emotions might otherwise lead to poor decisions. Include specific sections: your investment goals with target amounts and timelines, your assessed risk tolerance and the allocation it suggests, your chosen investments with specific fund names and ticker symbols, your re balancing frequency and thresholds, and your commitments about what you will not do such as panic selling, chasing performance, or making changes based on media predictions.

Write specific scenario-response pairs: "If my portfolio declines thirty percent, I will maintain all positions and continue regular contributions, recognizing that crashes create opportunities" and "If I feel tempted to chase a hot sector or stock getting media attention, I will review this policy statement and remember that index fund investing beats active management for most investors." Store this document somewhere easily accessible like a password manager or important documents folder, and commit to reviewing it before making any changes to your investment strategy to ensure decisions are based on your rational long-term plan rather than emotional short-term responses.

Quarterly Review Checklist:

Establish a quarterly review process that keeps you connected to your portfolio and investment progress without obsessive daily monitoring that increases anxiety and poor decision-making likelihood. Every quarter on a predetermined date, spend thirty minutes reviewing: account balances across all investment accounts, contributions made during the quarter, current asset allocation compared to targets, year-to-date performance compared to appropriate benchmarks, and any life changes that might affect your investment strategy or risk tolerance.

Document these quarterly reviews in a simple spreadsheet or notebook, tracking your net worth growth over time and noting any observations about your emotional reactions to market movements or changes in life circumstances affecting your financial plan. Use the review to celebrate progress when portfolio values increase and to remind yourself of your long-term strategy when values decline, reinforcing that quarterly and even annual performance matters far less than decades-long consistency in contributing and maintaining your allocation through market cycles.

Building a wealth portfolio is not about brilliant stock picking, perfect timing, or sophisticated strategies that require constant management; it's about choosing appropriate asset allocations, investing in low-cost diversified funds, maintaining discipline through market volatility, and contributing consistently regardless of market conditions. The investor who implements a simple three-fund portfolio, contributes five hundred dollars monthly for forty years, and re balances annually without panic selling will almost certainly outperform the investor who constantly adjusts strategy, chases performance, or abandons the plan during crashes despite having access to the same funds and similar resources. Simplicity, consistency, and discipline beat complexity, cleverness, and emotional decision-making in investing every single time over multi-decade periods.

12

Real Estate Investing - Building Wealth Through Property

Section 1: Your Primary Residence as Investment

The debate over whether your primary residence counts as an investment or simply an expense rages endlessly among personal finance experts, with compelling arguments on both sides that miss the nuanced reality that housing can be either depending on how you approach it and what alternatives you're comparing it against. Understanding the true economics of home ownership versus renting, including all costs and opportunity costs rather than just the simplistic mortgage-versus-rent comparison, helps you make rational decisions about housing based on building wealth rather than emotion or social pressure about achieving the supposed milestone of home ownership.

Buying versus renting represents far more than the simple calculation of mortgage payment compared to rent that most people use to justify home purchases without considering the full financial picture. The monthly payment comparison misleads because it ignores property taxes, insurance, maintenance, repairs, HOA fees, and the opportunity cost of capital tied up in down payments and home equity that could be invested elsewhere generating compound returns. A house with a two thousand dollar mortgage payment might cost three thousand monthly all-in when you add taxes, insurance, and maintenance, and that's before considering the hundred thousand dollar down payment that could have been invested earning ten percent annually.

The complete financial comparison requires calculating total monthly cost of ownership including mortgage principal and interest, property taxes, homeowners insurance, maintenance and repairs estimated at one to two percent of home value annually, HOA fees if applicable, and utilities that might be included in rent but paid separately in owned homes. This total often exceeds comparable rent by thirty to fifty percent or more, meaning the mortgage payment being less than rent doesn't automatically make buying cheaper when you account for all ownership costs that renters don't pay.

The additional consideration is opportunity cost of capital, calculating what the down payment and home equity could earn if invested in diversified portfolios instead of tied up in a house. Someone who puts one hundred thousand down on a house and builds two hundred thousand in equity over a decade through mortgage paydown and appreciation has three hundred thousand tied up in real estate. If that same three hundred thousand had been invested in diversified index funds over the same period, it would likely have grown to over five hundred thousand at typical market returns, suggesting an opportunity cost of two hundred thousand from having capital in the house rather than in financial assets.

Building equity through home ownership happens through two mechanisms: mortgage principal pay down that gradually converts debt to equity, and property appreciation that increases home value over time without requiring additional capital investment. The principal pay down is forced savings that makes home ownership attractive for people who struggle with investment discipline, as the monthly mortgage payment automatically builds equity rather than requiring separate decisions to invest. However, this forced savings comes at the cost of concentration risk from having too much wealth in a single asset and reduced flexibility compared to holding liquid investments.

Property appreciation provides the primary argument for viewing homes as investments rather than just expenses, as real estate has historically appreciated at roughly the rate of inflation over long periods, preserving purchasing power while providing shelter. In some markets and time periods, appreciation has exceeded inflation substantially, creating genuine wealth gains for homeowners who bought in the right places at the right times. However, this appreciation is far from guaranteed and many homeowners have seen property values decline or stagnate for years, particularly those who bought near market peaks in overvalued markets.

The reality is that home appreciation has averaged roughly three percent annually over very long periods, matching inflation and meaning real inflation-adjusted returns from appreciation alone are approximately zero. The actual return from home ownership comes primarily from the leverage effect of mortgage financing, where you control an asset worth several times your down payment and capture appreciation on the full value while only investing a fraction of it. Someone who puts one hundred thousand down on a five hundred thousand house and sees five percent appreciation gains twenty-five thousand in equity, a twenty-five percent return on their one hundred thousand invested capital despite just five percent property appreciation.

When renting is actually smarter than buying challenges the cultural narrative that home ownership is always the right financial decision and renting is "throwing money away," when the mathematical reality often favors renting for people in expensive markets, early in careers, or who value flexibility over forced savings. Renting makes financial sense when the total cost of ownership substantially exceeds comparable rent, when you expect to move within five years and won't recoup transaction costs, when local property values seem overvalued and likely to stagnate or decline, or when you'd rather invest capital in diversified assets than concentrate it in a single property.

The transaction costs of buying and selling homes including realtor commissions, closing costs, inspections, and other fees typically total eight to ten percent of home value, meaning you need approximately that much appreciation just to break even compared to renting. Someone who buys a five hundred thousand dollar home and sells five years later needs the property to appreciate to at least five hundred fifty thousand just to cover the transaction costs of buying and selling, making ownership unattractive compared to renting unless you're confident of appreciation exceeding two percent annually over your ownership period or you plan to stay long enough to spread transaction costs over many years.

Section 2: Rental Property Investing

Single-family versus multi-family properties present different risk-return profiles and management complexity levels, with single-family homes being simpler to finance and manage but offering less diversification than multi-family properties with multiple rent-paying units. Single-family rentals attract longer-term tenants, often families seeking stability, and tend to appreciate better in good markets because they compete with owner-occupied homes for buyers. However, vacancy in a single-family rental means zero income while fixed costs continue, creating periods of negative cash flow that can be devastating without adequate reserves.

Multi-family properties from duplexes through large apartment buildings provide tenant diversification that reduces vacancy risk, as losing one tenant in a fourplex means twenty-five percent vacancy rather than one hundred percent in a single-family. The economies of scale in maintenance and management make multi-family properties more efficient to operate per unit than managing scattered single-family rentals, as one roof repair covers multiple units and property management becomes cost-effective at smaller portfolio sizes. However, multi-family properties are more expensive requiring larger down payments, harder to finance as investment properties, and require more sophisticated management capabilities than single-family rentals.

Calculating cash flow and ROI requires understanding all the numbers beyond just rent minus mortgage, including vacancy reserves, maintenance costs, property management fees, property taxes, insurance, utilities, capital expenditure reserves, and the opportunity cost of capital invested. The simplified calculation many beginning investors use of just rent minus mortgage and basic expenses overstates actual returns by ignoring several thousand dollars in annual costs that are easy to overlook until they arrive. A rental property generating three thousand monthly in rent with a two thousand dollar mortgage might seem like great cash flow until you account for one month vacancy annually, property management taking ten percent of rent, maintenance averaging one percent of property value, property taxes and insurance of several hundred monthly, and capital expenditure reserves for eventual roof, HVAC, or other major replacements.

The more complete cash flow calculation might show that same property generating just three to six hundred monthly in actual sustainable cash flow after all expenses including reserves, or ten to twenty percent cash-on-cash return on a one hundred thousand dollar investment in down payment and reserves. This return is reasonable but less exciting than the simplistic calculation suggested, and it requires active management or paying for professional management that reduces returns further. The cash flow provides income but the real wealth building comes from mortgage paydown and appreciation over decades of ownership.

The one percent rule and fifty percent rule provide quick screening heuristics for evaluating potential rental properties, helping you eliminate obviously bad deals before spending time on detailed analysis. The one percent rule suggests monthly rent should be at least one percent of purchase price for a property to potentially cash flow positively after expenses, meaning a two hundred thousand dollar property should rent for at least two thousand monthly. Properties meeting this rule might work financially; properties far below this ratio almost certainly won't provide adequate returns to justify the investment and risk.

The fifty percent rule estimates that operating expenses including everything except mortgage will consume approximately fifty percent of gross rents, providing a simple way to estimate cash flow without detailed expense analysis. Using this rule, a property renting for three thousand monthly has approximately fifteen hundred in operating expenses and fifteen hundred remaining for mortgage payment, making properties with mortgage payments substantially exceeding half of rent unlikely to cash flow positively. These rules are imperfect and actual expenses vary by property and market, but they help you quickly eliminate deals that don't meet basic financial viability thresholds.

Finding and analyzing deals separates successful real estate investors who build portfolios from people who buy properties emotionally or without proper analysis and lose money through negative cash flow or poor appreciation. Finding deals means building relationships with real estate agents who understand investment properties and can alert you to listings meeting your criteria, searching MLS for properties that meet one percent rule screening, driving neighborhoods looking for distressed properties or FSBO signs, and networking with other investors who might have leads on off-market opportunities. The best deals often come from motivated sellers willing to negotiate on price or terms rather than perfectly listed properties at full market value.

Analyzing deals requires running detailed proforma projections of income and expenses over your expected holding period, calculating multiple return metrics including cash-on-cash return, cap rate, internal rate of return, and net present value to understand whether the property meets your investment criteria. Conservative analysis assumes higher expenses and vacancy than optimistic scenarios, uses realistic rather than best-case appreciation assumptions, and includes adequate reserves for capital expenditures and unexpected costs. The investors who succeed in real estate are those who walk away from ninety-nine deals that don't meet their criteria to buy the one that does, rather than forcing marginal deals because they're eager to get started.

Section 3: House Hacking Your Way to Wealth

Living in one unit while renting others represents perhaps the most powerful wealth-building strategy available to people willing to sacrifice some privacy and deal with tenant management while living in the same building as their renters. House hacking works by purchasing a multi-family property like a duplex, triplex, or fourplex with an owner-occupied loan requiring lower down payments than investment property loans, living in one unit while renting the others to tenants who cover most or all of your housing costs through their rent payments. This strategy can reduce your housing expense from perhaps two thousand monthly to zero or even positive cash flow while you build equity through tenants paying down your mortgage.

The mathematics are compelling for young people or families willing to accept reduced privacy: a fourplex purchased for five hundred thousand with three and a half percent down FHA loan has monthly payment of approximately twenty-eight hundred including principal, interest, taxes, and insurance. If three units rent for one thousand each, rental income of three thousand covers the entire mortgage plus some expenses, meaning you live essentially for free while building equity and gaining property management experience. After a year or two of owner-occupation meeting the loan requirement, you can move out and rent the fourth unit as well, converting the property to four thousand monthly rental income against the twenty-eight hundred mortgage for positive cash flow funding your next house hack purchase.

Accessory dwelling units allow single-family homeowners to house hack by adding legal secondary dwelling units to their properties through garage conversions, basement apartments, or backyard cottages that can be rented while you continue living in the main house. ADUs provide house hacking benefits of reduced housing costs through rental income while maintaining more privacy than sharing a duplex, as the ADU tenant has separate entrance and isn't sharing common areas or walls as directly. The rental income from an ADU can cover substantial portions of mortgage payments, potentially reducing monthly housing costs from two thousand to five hundred or less depending on local rental rates.

The investment required for ADU construction varies dramatically by location and project scope, ranging from thirty thousand for basic garage conversions to one hundred fifty thousand or more for new detached construction in expensive markets. This upfront cost requires either savings, cash-out refinancing, or home equity loans to fund, but the ongoing rental income of eight hundred to two thousand monthly depending on market provides solid returns that often exceed ten percent annually on the construction cost while simultaneously building home equity. Many cities have simplified ADU permitting and reduced fees to encourage housing creation, making ADU house hacking increasingly accessible to homeowners in single-family neighborhoods.

FHA loans and low down payments make house hacking accessible to people without substantial savings who couldn't otherwise afford investment property down payments of twenty to twenty-five percent. FHA loans allow owner-occupied multi-family purchases with just three and a half percent down payment, meaning a three hundred thousand duplex requires only ten thousand five hundred down payment compared to sixty to seventy-five thousand for conventional investment property financing. This low barrier to entry allows people in their twenties and thirties to begin building rental property portfolios years earlier than if they had to save conventional investment property down payments.

The requirements for FHA financing include owner-occupying the property for at least one year, meeting credit score minimums of typically five hundred eighty or higher, and limiting purchase price to FHA loan limits that vary by county but are often sufficient for multi-family properties in many markets. After the one-year owner-occupancy period, you can move out and rent all units while retaining the favorable low-down-payment FHA loan, then potentially repeat the process by purchasing another multi-family property with FHA financing for your new primary residence. This serial house hacking strategy can build portfolios of three to four multi-family properties over six to eight years with minimal total down payment investment.

The lifestyle trade-offs of house hacking include reduced privacy from living in the same building as tenants who might be noisy or create issues, responsibility for property management and maintenance that can interrupt evenings and weekends, and limitations on where you live dictated by available multi-family properties meeting investment criteria rather than choosing neighborhoods purely for lifestyle preferences. These trade-offs are substantial and not everyone is willing to accept them even for significant financial benefits, making house hacking a strategy that works better for some personality types and life stages than others.

Young single people or couples without children often find house hacking trade-offs completely acceptable in exchange for dramatically reduced housing costs and accelerated wealth building, viewing the tenant management and reduced privacy as temporary inconveniences during a few years of aggressive wealth building. Families with young children might find house hacking more challenging due to noise concerns, safety issues with tenants in close proximity, and the desire for stable housing rather than moving every year or two to the next house hack property. The decision requires honest assessment of your tolerance for the downsides balanced against the substantial financial benefits.

Section 4: Alternative Real Estate Investing

REITs provide real estate exposure through stock-like securities that trade on exchanges, allowing real estate investing without the capital requirements, management responsibilities, or concentration risk of direct property ownership. Real Estate Investment Trusts are companies that own and operate income-producing properties like apartments, office buildings, retail centers, warehouses, or specialized properties, distributing at least ninety percent of taxable income to shareholders as dividends. These dividends provide current income while REIT share prices can appreciate with property values and rental income growth, creating total return opportunities similar to direct property ownership.

The benefits of REIT investing include complete liquidity with ability to buy and sell shares instantly unlike properties that take months to sell, diversification across many properties and property types rather than concentration in one or few properties, no management responsibilities or tenant headaches, and access to commercial property types like office buildings or retail centers that individual investors can't realistically own directly. Someone with ten thousand dollars can invest in REITs and gain exposure to millions of dollars of diversified real estate, impossible through direct ownership requiring hundreds of thousands in capital per property.

The downsides of REITs compared to direct ownership include no leverage benefits unless the REIT itself uses leverage in its property acquisitions, no ability to add value through property improvements or better management, and tax treatment of dividends as ordinary income rather than preferential qualified dividend rates. The correlation of REIT prices with stock markets rather than local property markets means REITs sometimes decline when stocks decline even if underlying real estate values are stable, creating volatility that differs from direct property ownership that doesn't have daily price marks.

Real estate crowdfunding platforms like Fundrise, RealtyMogul, or Crowd-Street allow smaller investors to participate in specific real estate projects or diversified portfolios with minimum investments of five hundred to one thousand dollars, providing alternative access to real estate between direct ownership and REITs. These platforms pool investor money to purchase properties or provide debt financing to real estate developers, distributing rental income or interest payments to investors along with their share of eventual property sale proceeds. The appeal is access to institutional-quality real estate investments and returns that were historically available only to wealthy investors.

The structure varies by platform and investment, with some offering diversified portfolios selected and managed by the platform while others allow investors to choose specific properties or development projects to invest in. Some investments are relatively liquid with quarterly redemption windows, while others are liquid long-term holds of five to ten years with no ability to exit early. The returns typically target eight to twelve percent annually through a combination of current distributions and appreciation, competitive with direct ownership returns without the management responsibilities.

The risks of real estate crowdfunding include liquidity for many investments that lock up capital for years with no exit options, platform risk if the crowdfunding company itself fails or is poorly managed, limited transparency and control compared to direct ownership where you can inspect properties and make management decisions, and fees that can reduce returns by one to two percent annually. The regulatory structure is still evolving and investor protections are less developed than for stocks or mutual funds, making due diligence on platforms and specific investments crucial before committing capital.

Syndication and partnerships allow investors to pool money with others to purchase larger properties than they could afford individually, typically structured with general partners who manage the property and limited partners who are passive investors. A syndication might raise two million dollars from twenty limited partners contributing one hundred thousand each to purchase a ten million dollar apartment building with the remaining eight million from a loan, with general partners handling all management in exchange for performance fees and larger share of profits. This structure provides access to commercial properties and professional management while requiring much less capital than solo ownership.

The returns from syndication typically target fifteen to twenty percent annually through a combination of cash distributions during the holding period and share of sale proceeds after five to seven years when the property is sold. These returns exceed what most individual investors achieve from single-family rentals because of the economies of scale in commercial property management, the expertise of professional sponsors, and the leverage from commercial financing. However, the liquidity is complete with capital locked up for the full holding period, and the returns depend entirely on the sponsor's competence and honesty.

Commercial real estate basics including office buildings, retail centers, industrial warehouses, and other property types provide diversification from residential real estate and potentially higher returns through professional management and longer lease terms with business tenants. Commercial properties are valued based on net operating income divided by capitalization rates, creating more mathematical pricing than residential properties that depend heavily on comparable sales and buyer emotion. This cap rate valuation means improving net operating income through better management, higher rents, or reduced expenses directly increases property value by a multiple of the income increase.

The barriers to direct commercial real estate investing include much higher capital requirements typically requiring millions of dollars even with leverage, specialized knowledge needed to evaluate properties and leases, and different financing structures than residential properties. Most individual investors access commercial real estate through REITs, crowdfunding, or syndication rather than direct ownership, leaving direct commercial ownership to wealthy individuals or professional real estate investors with substantial capital and expertise.

Actionable Takeaways

Real estate investing transforms from abstract concept into actual wealth-building through specific actions that move you from studying and planning to owning properties that generate rental income and appreciate while tenants pay down mortgages. The difference between people who talk about real estate investing for years and those who build substantial portfolios is simply taking action despite uncertainty and fear, starting with first properties that might not be perfect but provide learning experiences and begin the wealth accumulation process. This quarter you need to take concrete steps toward real estate investing whether that's buying your first house hack property, investing in REITs through your brokerage account, or thoroughly analyzing your first potential rental deal.

Rental Property Calculator:

Create a comprehensive analysis spreadsheet for evaluating potential rental properties that calculates all return metrics and ensures you're accounting for all expenses rather than just the simplistic rent-minus-mortgage calculation that overstates returns. Build or download a template that includes purchase price, down payment amount and percentage, loan details including interest rate and term, estimated monthly rent, and all monthly expenses: property taxes, insurance, HOA fees, property management at ten percent of rent, maintenance at one percent of property value annually, vacancy reserve at one month annually, and capital expenditure reserve at half a percent of property value.

Calculate monthly and annual cash flow after all expenses, cash-on-cash return as annual cash flow divided by total cash invested including down payment and reserves, and sensitivity analysis showing how returns change if rents are lower than expected or expenses higher. Use this calculator to analyze every property you consider, walking away from any that don't meet your minimum return requirements rather than forcing deals because you're eager to get started. The discipline to say no to ninety-nine marginal deals to find the one that works is what separates successful real estate investors from those who lose money.

House Hacking Feasibility Worksheet:

Determine whether house hacking makes sense for your situation by calculating specific scenarios with real numbers from your local market and honest assessment of your tolerance for the lifestyle trade-offs. Research current listings for duplexes, triplexes, and fourplexes in areas where you'd be willing to live, noting typical purchase prices and what individual units rent for in similar properties. Calculate the all-in monthly cost including mortgage, taxes, insurance, and basic maintenance, then subtract rental income from the other units to determine your net housing cost or potential positive cash flow.

Compare this net cost to your current or alternative housing expense to see the monthly savings from house hacking, then multiply by twelve and by five or ten years to see the cumulative savings that could be invested toward additional properties or other wealth building. Honestly assess whether you'd be willing to live in the same building as tenants, handle maintenance issues and tenant management, and potentially move every year or two to new house hack properties during your accumulation phase. If the numbers work and you're willing to accept the trade-offs, begin serious planning including improving credit if needed, saving for down payment, and researching financing options.

REIT Investment Allocation:

If direct property ownership seems too capital-intensive, management-heavy, or risky for your current situation, implement real estate exposure through REITs in your investment portfolio providing diversification and real estate returns without the headaches of property management. Decide on an appropriate real estate allocation as a percentage of your total portfolio, typically ten to twenty percent depending on how much you already have in direct property ownership or real estate through other channels. With a one hundred thousand dollar portfolio and fifteen percent target REIT allocation, you'd invest fifteen thousand in REIT index funds or individual REITs.

Choose between broad REIT index funds that own shares of many REITs across property types, or individual REITs focused on specific property sectors like residential, retail, office, industrial, or specialized properties like healthcare facilities or cell towers. For most investors, broad REIT index funds like Vanguard's VNQ provide adequate diversification with minimal complexity and low fees, while more sophisticated investors might select individual REITs based on their views about different property sectors. Implement your REIT allocation in your next re balancing or through directing new contributions toward REIT funds until you reach your target percentage.

Real Estate Education Plan:

Commit to a systematic real estate education program over the next three to six months that builds knowledge and confidence without the endless studying that becomes procrastination preventing you from ever starting. Choose two to three high-quality books on real estate investing like "The Book on Rental Property Investing" by Brandon Turner, "The Millionaire Real Estate Investor" by Gary Keller, or "Building Wealth One House at a Time" by John Schaub, reading them thoroughly and taking detailed notes on key concepts and strategies.

Listen to real estate investing podcasts like Bigger Pockets during commutes or exercise, absorbing different perspectives and deal analyses from experienced investors without requiring dedicated study time. Attend local real estate investor meetups or online forums to network with others pursuing similar goals, learning from their successes and mistakes while building relationships with potential partners, contractors, or property managers. Set a specific deadline by which you'll complete your education and take action on your first investment whether that's purchasing a house hack property, investing in syndication, or building a REIT allocation in your portfolio.

Real estate investing provides powerful wealth-building opportunities through leverage, tax benefits, and potential appreciation combined with rental income, but it's not magic and not without risks including liquidity, concentration, management headaches, and potential for losses if you buy in overvalued markets or manage properties poorly. The investors who succeed in real estate are those who analyze properties conservatively, walk away from marginal deals, maintain adequate reserves for vacancies and repairs, and treat real estate as a business requiring management and attention rather than passive investment. Whether you build wealth through direct property ownership, house hacking, or indirect exposure through REITs and crowdfunding, real estate deserves consideration as a component of diversified wealth-building strategy alongside stocks and other assets.

13

Your Personalized Wealth Plan - Putting It All Together

Section 1: Your Financial Freedom Number

Understanding exactly how much wealth you need to achieve financial independence transforms the abstract goal of "being rich" into a concrete target you can work toward systematically, replacing vague hopes with specific numbers that guide your saving, investing, and lifestyle decisions. Most people never calculate their financial freedom number and therefore never know whether they're on track, off track, or how far away financial independence actually is based on their current trajectory. This lack of clarity keeps them working indefinitely without knowing if another year or another decade is required, missing opportunities to retire early because they didn't realize they'd already accumulated enough.

Calculating how much wealth you need starts with determining your annual spending in financial independence, the amount you'll need to withdraw from investments each year to fund your lifestyle without employment income. This isn't your current spending including mortgage payments that will be finished or work expenses that won't exist in retirement, but rather your actual living expenses adjusted for retirement reality. Someone currently spending seventy thousand annually might need only fifty thousand in retirement after eliminating mortgage, commuting costs, work clothes, and savings contributions that become spending instead.

The four percent rule for retirement represents the most widely used framework for determining how much you need to retire, suggesting you can safely withdraw four percent of your initial portfolio balance annually adjusted for inflation with very low risk of running out of money over thirty-year retirement periods. This rule comes from historical analysis showing that portfolios of fifty to seventy-five percent stocks weathered virtually all historical thirty-year periods including the Great Depression and multiple market crashes when using four percent initial withdrawal rates. The calculation is simple: divide your annual spending by four percent to determine your financial independence number.

Someone needing fifty thousand annually in retirement requires one point two-five million using the four percent rule, calculated as fifty thousand divided by point-zero-four equals one million two hundred fifty thousand. This portfolio would support fifty thousand in first-year withdrawals, increasing each subsequent year with inflation to maintain purchasing power, with historical analysis suggesting over ninety-five percent success rate of not depleting the portfolio over thirty years. The simplicity of this calculation makes financial independence planning accessible to anyone who can estimate their spending and do basic division.

The assumptions and debates about the four percent rule center on whether historical analysis applies to future market conditions, whether lower expected returns from stocks and bonds suggest more conservative withdrawal rates, and whether longer retirements spanning forty or fifty years require reducing withdrawal rates to three or three point five percent. Critics argue that current market valuations and low bond yields make four percent too aggressive, suggesting three to three point five percent provides more certainty of portfolio survival over very long retirement periods. This debate matters because reducing from four percent to three percent withdrawal rates increases required portfolio size by thirty-three percent.

The conservative investor concerned about portfolio depletion might target three percent withdrawals requiring one point six-seven million to support fifty thousand annual spending, while the aggressive investor comfortable with some risk might use four point five percent requiring just one point one million for the same spending. The truth is that no withdrawal rate guarantees success and all involve some risk of depletion or conversely leaving enormous estates you could have enjoyed during life. Most people should probably target something between three point five and four percent as reasonable balance between safety and not over saving to the point of unnecessarily delaying retirement.

FIRE movement principles of Financial Independence Retire Early represent an aggressive approach to wealth building through extreme saving rates, often fifty to seventy percent of income, with the goal of accumulating enough wealth to retire in their thirties or forties rather than working until traditional retirement age. The FIRE community has popularized financial independence planning and the four percent rule, demonstrating that retiring decades early is mathematically possible through high savings rates combined with modest living expenses. Someone saving seventy percent of a one hundred thousand income invests seventy thousand annually while living on thirty, potentially accumulating enough to support thirty thousand annual spending in just ten to fifteen years depending on market returns.

The various FIRE approaches include Lean FIRE with very low spending supported by minimal portfolio sizes, Fat FIRE with higher spending requiring larger portfolios, Barista FIRE with part-time work supplementing smaller portfolios, and Coast FIRE where you've accumulated enough that compound growth will reach your target by traditional retirement age even without additional contributions. These variations acknowledge that financial independence isn't binary and partial independence or reduced work is valuable even if you don't achieve complete independence from employment income.

Different levels of financial freedom beyond complete retirement include having enough passive income to cover basic expenses like housing and food even if you still need employment income for discretionary spending, accumulating enough wealth that work becomes optional and you could quit if desired even if you choose to continue, building sufficient investments that part-time work or lower-stress employment adequately supplements investment income, or reaching the point where investment income exceeds spending and wealth grows automatically without contributions. These intermediate milestones provide motivation and optionality before reaching complete financial independence.

Section 2: The One-Year Wealth Sprint

Month-by-month action plans transform overwhelming long-term wealth building into achievable near-term goals you can tackle systematically, building momentum through visible progress that motivates continued effort. Most people fail at wealth building not because the path is impossible but because they're overwhelmed by how far they need to go and give up before making meaningful progress. Breaking the journey into twelve monthly milestones creates a sense of accomplishment and control that sustains effort when the ultimate goal still feels distant.

The first quarter focuses on foundation building through the unglamorous work of assessing your current situation, eliminating obvious financial waste, and establishing the automated systems that make wealth building sustainable. Month one is your financial audit month where you calculate net worth, track all expenses for thirty days, list every debt with balances and rates, and assess your current savings rate as percentage of income. This reality check is uncomfortable but essential, providing the baseline against which all future progress gets measured and the clarity about what needs to change.

Month two implements the automatic wealth system by setting up proper account structures, establishing split direct deposit or automatic transfers to separate savings from spending, opening high-yield savings accounts and investment accounts if you don't have them, and automating retirement contributions to capture full employer match. These system implementations take just hours of setup time but provide value for years through making wealth building automatic rather than requiring constant willpower and decisions.

Month three begins debt elimination for people with consumer debt through choosing avalanche or snowball method, making first accelerated debt payments beyond minimums using money freed from expense cutting and automation, contacting credit card companies to negotiate lower rates, and setting specific targets for debt payoff over the next twelve to twenty-four months. The psychological lift from making real progress on debt during this month, even if modest, creates momentum that carries through the next phases.

The second quarter shifts from foundation to income acceleration, recognizing that earning more provides faster wealth building than endless expense optimization once you've cut major categories and automated saving. Month four focuses on maximizing primary income through documenting your work achievements, researching market rates for your role, preparing salary negotiation strategy and scripts, and either requesting raises or beginning strategic job searches if current employer won't pay market rates. Taking action on income rather than just accepting whatever you're paid separates people who build wealth quickly from those who optimize endlessly around modest incomes.

Month five launches your first income stream beyond primary employment, whether that's starting a side hustle, beginning freelancing, creating a service offering, or implementing another form of additional income generation. The goal isn't creating perfect businesses but rather starting imperfect income-generating activities that can be refined over time, overcoming the paralysis that keeps most people planning indefinitely without launching anything. Even modest side income of five hundred to one thousand monthly during the early months provides meaningful fuel for debt payoff or investing while building skills and confidence for potentially larger income streams.

Month six evaluates and optimizes your side income efforts based on three months of experience, doubling down on what's working while cutting activities that aren't generating acceptable returns relative to time invested. Many people dabble in multiple side hustles simultaneously and end up earning nothing from any of them because effort is too diffused, while focused effort on one or two most promising opportunities generates actual income. This month's optimization creates clarity about whether to continue building specific income streams or pivoting to different approaches.

The third quarter implements sophisticated tax and investment optimization that builds on the foundation created in earlier months. Month seven maximizes tax-advantaged account contributions by increasing 401k deferrals if not already maxed, opening and funding Roth IRA accounts, setting up HSA contributions if eligible, and implementing backdoor Roth strategies for high earners. The tax savings from these moves compounds over decades into hundreds of thousands of dollars, making them extraordinarily high-value activities despite requiring just hours to implement.

Month eight builds your investment portfolio by selecting appropriate asset allocation based on age and risk tolerance, choosing specific low-cost index funds for each asset class, making initial investments if new to investing or re balancing if you already have portfolios, and automating monthly contributions so investing happens consistently without requiring ongoing decisions. The combination of right allocations, low-cost funds, and automated contributions creates the foundation for decades of wealth accumulation.

Month nine implements advanced strategies including tax-loss harvesting in taxable accounts, reviewing asset location to ensure tax-efficient placement of different assets across account types, optimizing charitable giving through bunching or appreciated stock donations if applicable, and exploring real estate investing options through REITs or evaluating house hacking feasibility. These advanced moves provide incremental improvements that add up to meaningful additional returns over time.

The fourth quarter focuses on solidifying habits and planning for long-term sustainability beyond the intense one-year sprint. Month ten conducts comprehensive review of progress across all areas including net worth growth, debt reduction achieved, savings rate improvements, income increases implemented, and investment returns relative to appropriate benchmarks. This review provides motivation through visible progress and identifies areas needing additional attention in the coming year.

Month eleven develops your three-year and five-year wealth building plans with specific targets for net worth, annual income, debt elimination completion, emergency fund adequacy, and investment portfolio growth. These longer-term plans provide direction for continued progress after the initial sprint while acknowledging that the first year lays groundwork that accelerates progress in subsequent years through compound growth and established systems.

Month twelve creates your sustainable ongoing wealth building routine that maintains progress without the intensity of the initial sprint, establishing quarterly rather than monthly reviews, planning annual updates to investment strategy and tax optimization, scheduling annual salary negotiations or job market assessments, and committing to continuous income development through skills advancement or business growth. The goal is creating permanent wealth-building habits that continue indefinitely rather than just executing a one-time improvement project.

Quick wins versus long-term strategies acknowledges that some wealth building actions create immediate results while others require years to pay off, with optimal plans balancing both for sustained motivation and maximum cumulative impact. Quick wins include capturing full 401k employer match, cutting unused subscriptions, negotiating lower credit card rates, and switching to high-yield savings accounts, all providing immediate financial improvements requiring minimal ongoing effort. These wins build confidence and free up cash flow that funds longer-term strategies requiring patient execution.

Long-term strategies like building rental property portfolios, developing significant side businesses that replace employment income, accumulating seven-figure investment portfolios through decades of contributions, and completely eliminating six-figure debt loads require years of consistent effort without dramatic short-term results. These strategies ultimately create the most wealth but require sustaining motivation through years when progress feels slow, which is why balancing them with quick wins that provide regular positive feedback helps maintain commitment to the long game.

Section 3: The Five-Year Wealth Building Plan

Income growth milestones provide concrete targets for increasing earning power through strategic career moves, business development, multiple income stream creation, and skills advancement that commands higher compensation. The difference between someone earning fifty thousand at year five and someone earning one hundred thousand compounds over entire careers into millions of dollars in additional lifetime income, making income development one of the highest-return activities despite being harder than expense cutting or investment optimization.

Year one income targets might focus on capturing quick wins through salary negotiations for ten to fifteen percent raises, starting first side income generating three hundred to five hundred monthly, or making strategic job changes that increase compensation by twenty percent or more. These year-one moves establish upward income trajectory and build confidence in your ability to increase earning power rather than accepting whatever employers choose to pay.

Year two and three income goals escalate through scaling side income to one thousand to two thousand monthly or potentially replacing employment income if business growth warrants transition, achieving promotions or lateral moves increasing base compensation by another fifteen to twenty percent, and developing valuable skills through certifications, training, or experience that position you for future income jumps. By year three, your total income from all sources should be meaningfully higher than year zero, perhaps thirty to fifty percent depending on starting point and opportunities.

Year four and five income objectives might include transitioning to full entrepreneurship if side businesses have grown sufficiently, reaching senior-level compensation in your career field through demonstrated value and strategic positioning, or building portfolio income from rental properties or dividend-paying investments that supplement earned income. The goal is five-year income at least double the starting point through some combination of raises, career advancement, business income, and investment income.

Net worth targets by year establish wealth accumulation goals that account for starting position, income levels, savings rates, and expected investment returns, providing measures of progress beyond just focusing on income or expenses. Someone starting at negative fifty thousand net worth should target neutral to slightly positive by year one through debt payoff, one hundred thousand by year three through continued debt elimination and aggressive saving, and two hundred fifty thousand by year five through high savings rates and market returns on growing investment balances.

These targets necessarily vary dramatically based on starting point and income levels, with high earners able to accumulate wealth much faster than people with modest incomes, but the principle of setting specific numeric targets and tracking actual progress against them remains universally valuable. Someone who started with two hundred thousand net worth might target doubling to four hundred thousand in five years, while someone starting from zero might target one hundred fifty thousand. The specific numbers matter less than having clear targets and holding yourself accountable to making progress toward them.

Investment portfolio benchmarks track the growth of your invested assets separate from net worth that includes home equity and other less liquid wealth, providing focus on financial assets that generate returns and fund eventual financial independence. Year one might target establishing diversified portfolios with appropriate allocations even if balances remain modest, year two reaching first significant milestone like twenty-five or fifty thousand in investment accounts, year three implementing advanced strategies like tax-loss harvesting and asset location optimization, and year five reaching one hundred fifty to three hundred thousand in investment portfolios depending on income and savings rates.

The portfolio growth comes from three sources: monthly contributions from current income, employer matching and profit sharing in retirement accounts, and investment returns on accumulated balances. Early years see most growth from contributions as balances are small and returns on modest amounts don't move the needle much, while later years see investment returns becoming increasingly significant contributors to growth as balances grow large enough that even modest percentage returns represent substantial dollar amounts.

Skill development timeline plans advancement of knowledge and capabilities that increase earning power and create opportunities, whether through formal credentials, informal learning, or experience in high-value domains. Year one might focus on identifying highest-value skills for your field and beginning systematic learning through courses, books, or practice, year two earning relevant certifications or demonstrating new capabilities through work projects, year three becoming recognized for specific expertise that commands premium compensation, and year five achieving mastery level capabilities that position you for leadership roles or independent high-value consulting.

The specific skills depend entirely on your field and goals, with software developers focusing on emerging technologies or architecture capabilities, marketers building data analysis and growth strategy expertise, managers developing leadership and organizational design skills, and tradespeople mastering advanced techniques or business management. The key is strategic focus on skills that genuinely increase your market value rather than random learning that's interesting but doesn't translate to higher income.

Section 4: The Ten-Year Vision

Complete financial independence represents the ultimate wealth goal for most people, accumulating enough assets that investment returns cover all living expenses and work becomes optional rather than necessary for financial survival. The ten-year timeframe provides realistic horizon for people in their twenties through forties to potentially achieve financial independence through aggressive saving and investing, requiring sacrifice and discipline but delivering freedom decades earlier than traditional retirement.

Someone in their thirties earning eighty thousand and saving sixty percent invests forty-eight thousand annually, potentially accumulating seven hundred thousand to one million dollars over ten years depending on market returns. Using conservative four percent withdrawal rate, this supports twenty-eight to forty thousand in annual spending, achieving financial independence if they can live on that amount. This requires both high income and low spending but demonstrates that complete independence in ten years is mathematically possible for people willing to make extreme trade-offs.

For most people, the ten-year vision is partial financial independence where investment income covers significant portion of expenses rather than complete independence, creating options to work part-time, take lower-paying interesting work, or change careers without financial stress. Someone accumulating five hundred thousand in ten years generates twenty thousand annually at four percent withdrawal rates, covering substantial expenses even if not complete independence, dramatically improving life quality and reducing work requirements.

Business equity or exit strategies recognize that many people building wealth through entrepreneurship reach financial independence through selling businesses rather than accumulating investment portfolios, with successful business sales creating liquidity events that instantly achieve independence. Someone building a business to one million in annual revenue might sell for two to three million or more depending on profitability and industry multiples, creating complete financial independence from a single transaction rather than decades of portfolio accumulation.

The ten-year business building path requires different strategies than investing portfolios, focusing on developing valuable intellectual property or systems that make businesses sell able, building customer relationships and recurring revenue that survives founder departure, and systematically increasing revenue and profitability that drives valuation multiples. Not every business is sell able and many entrepreneurs find their businesses are too dependent on them personally to attract buyers, making deliberate work to build transferable value essential for eventual exits.

Real estate portfolio building over ten years can create substantial wealth through accumulated rental properties, either providing significant monthly cash flow that covers living expenses or building equity that can be accessed through refinancing or sales. Someone house hacking every two years and keeping properties as rentals after moving out could own four or five rental properties by year ten, generating potentially three to five thousand monthly in total cash flow after expenses while building equity through tenant-paid mortgages and appreciation.

The combination of cash flow and equity makes real estate an attractive ten-year wealth building path for people willing to accept property management responsibilities and the work required to find good deals. Someone with five rentals generating one thousand monthly each has five thousand monthly passive income or sixty thousand annually, potentially achieving financial independence if their spending fits within that income or at minimum having significant passive income supplementing other sources.

Legacy and generational wealth thinking extends the ten-year plan beyond personal financial independence to consider wealth transfer to children or charitable causes, shifting from accumulation for personal benefit to building resources that outlive you. This perspective changes some decisions about spending versus saving, encouraging somewhat higher saving rates to build estates that provide for multiple generations rather than spending everything during your lifetime for personal enjoyment.

The generational wealth approach might mean targeting three to five million rather than just one to two million needed for personal independence, accumulating excess specifically for children's inheritance or philanthropic purposes. This requires sacrifice of current consumption but creates potential to change your family's trajectory for generations, breaking cycles of financial stress and giving descendants opportunities you might not have had through inherited wealth or education funding.

Actionable Takeaways

Your personalized wealth plan transforms from abstract long-term vision into specific actionable road map through concrete implementation of the frameworks and timelines covered in this chapter, creating clarity about where you're going and how you'll get there. Most people never create written plans and therefore drift through their financial lives without clear direction, wondering why they're not making progress toward goals they never specifically defined or committed to achieving. This month you need to calculate your numbers, set your targets, and create the written plan that guides all future financial decisions.

Financial Freedom Number Calculator:

Determine your specific financial independence target by systematically calculating annual spending needs and dividing by your chosen withdrawal rate, creating concrete numbers to work toward rather than vague hopes of someday being rich. First, calculate your current annual spending across all categories, then adjust for retirement reality by eliminating mortgage payments if you expect to pay off your home, eliminating savings and investment contributions that become spending in retirement, reducing or eliminating work-related expenses like commuting and professional clothes, and potentially adjusting for geographic arbitrage if you plan to move to lower-cost areas in retirement.

Second, decide on your withdrawal rate between three and four percent based on your risk tolerance and desired safety margin, using four percent for standard planning, three point five percent for conservative approach, or three percent for maximum safety especially if planning very early retirement before traditional age. Third, divide your adjusted annual spending by your chosen withdrawal rate to calculate your financial independence number. Someone needing sixty thousand annually at four percent withdrawal rate requires one point five million, while using three point five percent requires one point seven-one million.

One-Year Action Plan Template:

Create month-by-month specific actions for your wealth building sprint, assigning concrete tasks to each month rather than vague intentions to generally improve your finances. Use the framework from section two but personalize it for your specific situation, perhaps accelerating certain phases if you've already completed foundation work or extending others if you're starting from very difficult circumstances. Write specific measurable targets for each month like "reduce monthly expenses by five hundred dollars through cutting subscriptions and downsizing apartment" or "increase 401k contribution t fifteen percent to capture full match plus additional deferral."

Review your action plan weekly to ensure you're completing monthly milestones, adjusting as needed when life interferes but maintaining overall commitment to the one-year sprint. Share your plan with accountability partner or spouse to create external motivation and support for difficult changes, and schedule monthly check-ins to review progress and plan the next month's specific actions. The written plan transforms abstract goals into concrete actions that fit into your calendar and to-do list.

Five-Year Milestone Tracker:

Build systematic tracking of major wealth building milestones over five years including net worth targets, income goals, debt elimination dates, and key skill development achievements. Create simple spreadsheet with rows for each metric and columns for current state plus targets at years one through five, filling in specific numbers for each milestone. For net worth, you might target starting at negative twenty thousand, reaching positive fifty thousand year one, one hundred fifty thousand year two, two hundred seventy-five thousand year three, four hundred twenty-five thousand year four, and six hundred thousand year five.

For income, you might target total annual income from all sources starting at sixty thousand, reaching seventy thousand year one through raises and small side income, eighty-five thousand year two, one hundred five thousand year three, one hundred thirty thousand year four, and one hundred sixty thousand year five through combination of career advancement, business growth, and investment income. Update this tracker quarterly with actual results, celebrating when you exceed targets and analyzing when you fall short to understand whether you need to adjust strategies or just maintain patience through temporary setbacks.

Ten-Year Vision Board Worksheet:

Define your ten-year vision across multiple dimensions including wealth accumulation, lifestyle design, work situation, and legacy goals, creating comprehensive picture of what financial independence means for your specific situation and values. Write detailed description of your life at year ten including where you live and what kind of housing you occupy, whether you're still working and if so what kind of work in what capacity, how you spend typical weeks with freed time from financial independence, what causes or people you're supporting with your wealth, and what your net worth and various income streams look like.

Make this vision specific and personal rather than generic financial independence descriptions, including details about hobbies you'll pursue, relationships you'll invest in, places you'll visit, and contributions you'll make. This vivid vision provides motivation during difficult years when progress feels slow and sacrifices feel burdensome, reminding you why you're building wealth rather than just consuming everything you earn. Review and update your ten-year vision annually as circumstances change and you refine your understanding of what financial freedom means to you.

Your personalized wealth plan provides the road map from current reality to financial freedom, transforming overwhelming long-term goals into achievable milestones you can work toward systematically. The specific numbers and timelines in your plan will differ from examples in this chapter based on your income, expenses, current wealth, and goals, but the principle of having written specific targets with concrete action plans remains universally essential. Wealthy people became wealthy not through vague hopes of someday being rich but through specific plans executed consistently despite obstacles and setbacks, maintaining focus on long-term vision while taking short-term actions that compound into extraordinary results over decades.

14

CONCLUSION: Your Wealthy Life Starts Today

The Commitment Required for Real Wealth

Let's be brutally honest about what stands between you and the financial freedom you claim to want: not your income level, not your circumstances, not the economy or your background or any of the external factors you've probably blamed for your financial situation. What stands between you and wealth is the commitment to do what wealthy people do consistently over years and decades, making decisions that prioritize long-term freedom over short-term comfort, delayed gratification over immediate pleasure, and strategic thinking over emotional reactions.

This commitment is not comfortable, glamorous, or easy, which is precisely why most people never make it despite knowing intellectually what they should do. Reading this entire book means nothing if you close it, nod appreciatively at the good ideas, and then continue living exactly as you were before, spending every dollar you earn, avoiding the uncomfortable conversations about raises, procrastinating on opening investment accounts, and choosing today's small pleasures over tomorrow's financial freedom.

Knowledge without action is just entertainment, and you've been entertained enough.

The commitment required starts this week, not next month or after you pay off that one thing or when circumstances are more favorable. This week you will complete your financial audit calculating exact net worth and tracking every expense. This week you will set up automatic transfers splitting your income between spending and wealth building before you have the chance to spend it all. This week you will open investment accounts if you don't have them and make your first investments if you've been sitting in cash paralyzed by fear or perfectionism. This week you will take one concrete action toward increasing your income whether that's requesting a raise conversation, reaching out to potential freelance clients, or researching properties for house hacking.

These actions will feel uncomfortable, scary, and premature because you don't feel ready, don't have all the answers, and worry about making mistakes. This discomfort is exactly the point, because every wealthy person you admire felt exactly the same way when they started but they took action anyway and learned through doing rather than waiting for perfect knowledge that never comes. The difference between wealthy people and broke people isn't intelligence, education, or even opportunity; it's the willingness to take action despite uncertainty and maintain that action through years when results feel inadequate compared to effort invested.

The sacrifices required for wealth building are real and substantial, and anyone claiming otherwise is selling something or doesn't understand what actual wealth building requires. You will sacrifice restaurants and entertainment that friends enjoy while you're eating at home and investing the difference. You will sacrifice new cars and trendy apartments for reliable used vehicles and adequate cheaper housing while redirecting that money toward assets that appreciate. You will sacrifice evenings and weekends for side hustles or skills development while others relax and complain about never having money. You will sacrifice the social approval that comes from visible consumption for the private satisfaction of watching net worth grow toward financial independence.

These sacrifices are temporary, typically lasting five to fifteen years of intense focus depending on your starting point, income, and goals, but they're non-negotiable for people starting without inherited wealth or extraordinary income. The question isn't whether you'll sacrifice; you'll sacrifice either way, either choosing temporary sacrifice of consumption for eventual freedom or accepting permanent sacrifice of freedom for temporary consumption. Choose consciously rather than defaulting to the path of least resistance that keeps you trapped in financial stress forever.

Progress Over Perfection

The perfectionism that keeps most people stuck in planning rather than executing stems from fear dressed up as thoroughness, using the excuse of wanting to do things right to avoid the discomfort and risk of actually doing them at all. You will never have perfect knowledge, perfect circumstances, or perfect plans, and waiting for those conditions means waiting forever while people with inferior knowledge and circumstances build wealth through imperfect action executed consistently.

Your first investments will probably be in slightly sub optimal funds at slightly wrong times, and that's completely fine because mediocre investments held for decades crush perfect investments you never make because you were still researching. Your first salary negotiation might be clumsy and result in a smaller raise than optimal execution would have achieved, but that clumsy five percent raise beats the zero percent raise from never having the conversation. Your first rental property might not be the best deal available if you'd searched another six months, but owning an adequate property that cash flows beats analyzing deals forever without buying anything.

The wealth you build through imperfect action executed immediately dwarfs the theoretical wealth you might have built through perfect action you keep planning but never executing. Someone who starts investing five hundred monthly today in reasonable index funds will have far more wealth in thirty years than someone who spends those same thirty years perfecting their investment strategy but never actually investing. The person who asks for a raise using an imperfect script this month will earn more over their career than the person who's still crafting the perfect negotiation approach five years from now.

This emphasis on action over perfection doesn't mean being reckless or making major decisions without research, but it does mean setting clear deadlines for research and planning phases, then taking action when those deadlines arrive regardless of whether you feel completely ready. Commit to making your first investment within two weeks of finishing this book even if you're still uncertain about optimal fund selection. Schedule your raise conversation within one month even if your pitch isn't perfectly polished. Start your side hustle within sixty days even if your business plan isn't complete.

The learning from imperfect action is invaluable and impossible to achieve through endless planning, because action surfaces problems and questions you couldn't have anticipated through research alone, forcing you to develop capabilities that planning never builds. You'll learn more about investing from watching your first portfolio drop twenty percent and maintaining discipline than from reading ten more books about volatility. You'll learn more about negotiation from one clumsy raise conversation than from watching hours of negotiation videos. You'll learn more about business from serving your first difficult client than from another month of business planning.

This action-based learning compounds over time as you refine your approaches based on real feedback rather than theoretical optimization, building genuine expertise through experience rather than just knowledge through study. The person who's been investing imperfectly for ten years understands markets and their own psychology in ways that someone who's been studying investing for ten years without actually investing cannot match. The person who's been negotiating imperfectly for their career understands leverage and positioning in ways that someone who's read extensively about negotiation but never actually done it will never grasp.

Wealth as Freedom, Not Just Money

The ultimate purpose of building wealth isn't accumulating the largest possible net worth or achieving some arbitrary definition of rich that impresses others with numbers on statements they'll never see. Wealth building is about creating freedom, options, and security that allow you to live life on your terms rather than being trapped by financial necessity into jobs you hate, relationships you've outgrown, or locations you want to leave.

Financial freedom means having enough assets that you could stop working if you chose to, even if you actually enjoy your work and choose to continue, because the optionality of knowing you don't need the job fundamentally changes your relationship with work and employers. You negotiate more effectively when you genuinely don't need this particular job. You take more risks and speak more honestly when losing the job wouldn't devastate you financially. You pursue meaningful work rather than just lucrative work when investment income covers basics and employment income becomes enhancement rather than necessity.

The freedom extends beyond just work to every domain of life where money creates or removes options. Freedom to leave toxic relationships rather than staying for financial security. Freedom to move to places you want to live rather than where job markets demand. Freedom to pursue education, creative projects, or entrepreneurship without needing immediate income. Freedom to be generous with family and causes you care about. Freedom to take time off when life demands it without financial catastrophe. Freedom to make decisions based on what's right rather than what you can afford.

This freedom doesn't require tens of millions or private jets to be valuable and life-changing. Someone with five hundred thousand invested has options and security that someone living paycheck to paycheck regardless of income level simply doesn't have, even though five hundred thousand won't fund elaborate lifestyles or early retirement for most people. Someone with one million has genuine financial independence in many scenarios even if they're not Manhattan-penthouse rich. The freedom comes in stages with each hundred thousand providing incrementally more options and security, making the journey valuable long before reaching ultimate destinations.

The paradox is that building this freedom requires sacrificing the feeling of freedom in the short term, living below your means and working harder than financially necessary to build assets that will eventually provide the real freedom you're temporarily sacrificing. Many people reject this trade-off, choosing immediate freedom to spend everything they earn rather than temporary discipline for eventual financial independence, then wondering why they remain trapped in jobs and locations they dislike because they can't afford to leave.

Your Unique Definition of Rich

The word "rich" means something different to every person reading this book, and the first step in actually becoming rich by your definition is explicitly defining what that means rather than pursuing some generic vision of wealth that might not even align with your values or provide satisfaction when achieved. For some people, rich means never worrying about bills or basic expenses, living comfortably without financial stress even if not extravagantly. For others, it means having specific experiences like traveling the world or living in particular places. For others, it means building generational wealth that changes their family's trajectory.

Your definition of rich should be personal enough to genuinely motivate you through years of sacrifice and discipline, specific enough to know when you've achieved it rather than perpetually chasing more, and honest enough to reflect what you actually want rather than what society or peer pressure suggests you should want. The person who defines rich as never worrying about bills needs far less wealth than the person who defines it as owning multiple homes and traveling first class, and neither definition is more valid than the other as long as it's genuinely yours rather than someone else's expectation.

Take time now to write your specific definition of what being rich means to you, including the dollar amounts required, the lifestyle it enables, the freedom it provides, and the security it creates. This definition becomes your North Star, guiding decisions about how much to earn, save, and invest while providing the finish line that lets you know when you've won the game and can shift from accumulation to enjoyment or legacy. Without this clear definition, you'll perpetually chase more regardless of how much you accumulate, never feeling wealthy despite achieving financial success by any objective measure.

The definition can and should evolve as you age and circumstances change, with what feels like rich in your twenties seeming inadequate in your forties as income and lifestyle expectations change. Revisit and update your definition periodically, but resist the temptation to continuously raise the bar as you approach previous targets, because perpetual target inflation means never actually achieving the freedom you're ostensibly building wealth to obtain. At some point you need to declare victory and shift from accumulation to enjoyment and legacy.

The Ripple Effect of Your Financial Success

Your journey to financial independence creates effects far beyond your personal benefit, influencing family, friends, colleagues, and potentially countless others through example, generosity, and the confidence that comes from taking control of your financial life. Most people never see anyone in their immediate circle achieve financial independence through deliberate saving and investing, making the entire concept feel abstract and impossible rather than concrete and achievable through systematic execution of known strategies.

Your success proves to everyone watching that financial independence is possible for regular people through deliberate action rather than luck, inheritance, or exceptional income. Your family members see that wealth building is achievable and may begin their own journeys inspired by your example. Your friends who've been stuck in financial stress see a path forward and the specific steps required. Your colleagues notice your confidence and changed relationship with work that comes from financial security. Your children if you have them learn healthy money habits and belief in their ability to build wealth through watching your behaviors.

This ripple effect extends through time as your children or mentees apply lessons learned from watching you, then pass those lessons to their children or mentees, creating generational change that outlives you. The person you help escape debt who then helps someone else who then helps another creates exponential impact that multiplies far beyond your direct actions. The financial security you build might enable generosity through time, money, or expertise that changes lives in ways you'll never fully know about.

The responsibility that comes with this potential impact is taking your wealth building seriously rather than giving up when progress feels slow or sacrifices feel hard, because your failure to achieve financial independence doesn't just hurt you but also removes the example and potential future help you could have provided to others. The world doesn't need another person who knows what they should do financially but doesn't actually do it; the world needs people who take action, achieve results, and demonstrate that financial freedom is possible through consistent execution of proven strategies.

Your Final Challenge: Take One Action Today

Everything you've learned across these thirteen chapters means absolutely nothing until you take action, translating knowledge into behaviors that actually change your financial trajectory. The gap between people who build wealth and people who remain broke despite knowing what to do is not knowledge; it's action, the willingness to do what needs doing despite discomfort, uncertainty, and fear.

Your challenge, starting right now before you close this book or move to the next item on your to-do list, is taking one concrete action toward building wealth. Not planning to take action or thinking about taking action or adding action to some future to-do list, but actually doing something in the next hour that moves you measurably closer to financial freedom.

Here are specific actions you can complete today:

Calculate your exact net worth by listing all assets and liabilities, creating the baseline against which all future progress gets measured. This takes thirty minutes and provides clarity about your starting point that removes the confusion and avoidance that keeps you stuck.

Set up automatic transfers from checking to savings account starting with your next paycheck, even if just fifty or one hundred dollars per paycheck, establishing the pay-yourself-first automation that makes wealth building sustainable rather than dependent on willpower that will eventually fail.

Open a brokerage account at Vanguard, Fidelity, or Schwab if you don't have one, completing the application that takes ten minutes and removes the friction preventing you from investing. Having the account doesn't commit you to perfect investment strategy but it eliminates the setup barrier that might otherwise delay you for months.

Make your first investment of any amount, even just one hundred dollars, in a total market index fund, overcoming the psychological barrier between knowing you should invest and actually being an investor who owns appreciating assets.

Email your manager requesting a conversation about compensation and your performance, taking the first step toward salary negotiation that could increase your income by thousands or tens of thousands annually.

Research and reach out to one potential client or customer for a side business or freelancing service you could offer, beginning the process of creating additional income streams beyond your primary employment.

Cancel three subscriptions or memberships you're not actively using, freeing up monthly cash flow you can redirect toward debt payoff or investing without reducing anything you actually value.

Calculate your financial independence number using the four percent rule, determining exactly how much wealth you need to achieve freedom so you have a concrete target to work toward rather than vague aspirations.

Schedule specific calendar time this week to complete three more actions from this list, ensuring that today's momentum continues rather than being a isolated burst of enthusiasm that fades without sustaining progress.

Choose one action from this list and do it now. Not tomorrow, not this weekend, not when you finish the other things you need to do first. Now. Because the distance between where you are financially and where you want to be will never close until you bridge it with action, and action delayed is wealth deferred.

The Beginning of Your Wealth-Building Journey

You've reached the end of this book but the beginning of your wealth-building journey, equipped with knowledge, frameworks, and action plans that provide everything you need to transform your financial life over the coming years and decades. The path forward is clear, the strategies are proven, and the only remaining question is whether you'll actually walk the path or just appreciate the map while remaining stuck where you started.

Ten years from today you'll be somewhere financially based on decisions you make starting now. You'll either have built substantial wealth through consistent execution of the strategies in this book, positioned yourself well on the path to financial independence, and fundamentally changed your relationship with money and work. Or you'll be essentially where you are now, perhaps earning more but spending more, knowing what you should have done but never quite getting around to doing it, still talking about someday being financially free.

The difference between these two futures is the decision you make right now about whether knowledge becomes action or remains theoretical understanding that makes you feel informed but doesn't change outcomes. Thousands of people will read this book, agree with its principles, and do nothing differently, joining the masses who perpetually consume personal finance content without ever actually building wealth. A small percentage will read this book and immediately begin executing, making uncomfortable changes, taking imperfect action, and building wealth through consistency rather than brilliance.

Which person will you be? The decision is yours, and the time to make it is now. Your wealthy life is waiting, but it won't come find you through hoping, wishing, or planning. It will come through doing, through taking action despite fear, through maintaining discipline when motivation fades, and through believing you deserve financial freedom enough to pay the price required to achieve it.

The clock is ticking. Your financial future is being determined by today's decisions. And everything you need to build the wealth you want is already in your hands.

Now go build it.

www.ingramcontent.com/pod-product-compliance
Lightning Source LLC
LaVergne TN
LVHW052304200926
848481LV00002B/463